THE NEW GREAT GAME

Proceedings of the Central Asia Symposium
Monterey, California
August 7-11, 2005

Central Asia Regional Security Issues, Economic and Political Challenges

Sponsored by the Foreign Military Studies Office,
Fort Leavenworth, Kansas,
and the Deputy Chief of Staff for Intelligence,
U.S. Army Training and Doctrine Command,
Fort Monroe, Virginia

Published by Books Express Publishing

ISBN 978-1-780390-47-5
To purchase copies at discounted prices please contact
info@books-express.com

Table of Contents

Part II—Issues and Concerns

PART III—The Way Ahead

Preface

The importance of Central Asia to three major powers—the United States, China, and Russia—is well understood but not widely recognized or discussed. Involvement in the region by the United States has been spotty and uneven over many years, but since 9.11 has taken on renewed importance in the War Against Terrorists. Russia views the region as its traditional sphere of influence, and the many strong ties between Russia and countries in Central Asia, especially Kazakhstan, reinforce this view. China has had a presence in the region via trade routes for centuries, but has only recently made a concerted effort to apply its influence.

Key issues for the area include the following: terrorism/transnational crime/drug trafficking, energy resources (oil and gas), trade, stable governance, border disputes, the role of cooperative security organizations (mainly the Shanghai Cooperation Organization, but there are a score of others), and, particularly, cooperation by the major powers.

The Foreign Military Studies Office (FMSO) engaged Russia's civilian and military experts over security concerns in this area often during the past decade. The August 2005 Central Asian Symposium, held in Monterey California, was a way for FMSO to gain a different and uniquely Chinese perspective on the area's problems and potential solutions. The timing and topic of the symposium are important, for China is growing more interested in Central Asia and its resources by the day. The region is less contentious than the Taiwan issue, however, and this factor increased the level of open discussion and value of the symposium dramatically. FMSO invited several top-rank Chinese researchers and analysts to attend the symposium, and also younger analysts/researchers with fresh perspectives on the region.

I hope the reader will enjoy the papers and discussion points included in this book. We highly value the contributions made by our Chinese guests and look forward to working with them again in the near future on aspects of the same topic.

March 10, 2006

Jacob W. Kipp
Director
FMSO

Acknowledgments

The primary sponsor for this work was Dr. Jacob Kipp, director of the Foreign Military Studies Office (FMSO) at Fort Leavenworth, Kansas, a subordinate unit of the U.S. Army's Training and Doctrine Command (TRADOC). The symposium's goal was to engage and network with Chinese scholars, researchers and analysts on a region of great interest to the U.S. and China—Central Asia. Ten Chinese Central Asian scholars agreed to attend and contribute chapters to this volume. The eleventh contributor, Brigadier General (retired) Feroz Khan of the Pakistan Army, currently a senior fellow at the U.S. Naval Postgraduate School (NPS), graciously allowed his symposium keynote address to be included as the first chapter in this work. This symposium was hosted by FMSO at the Hilton Hotel in Monterey, California, from August 7-11, 2005.

The event's success is attributable not only to FMSO but also to the contributions of the event's Chinese and American participants. Special recognition is owed to several senior Chinese researchers and officials. Mr. Zhuang Jianzhong, secretary general of the Shanghai Society for Rim of the Pacific Economic Development, provided access and introductions to important individuals at the Shanghai Academy of Social Sciences (SASS), including the head of the Central Asian and Russian Studies Department, Dr. Pan Guang. Mr. Rong Ying, vice president of the prestigious China Institute for International Studies (CIIS) in Beijing, helped ensure the attendance of Dr. Yang Shu, vice president and professor at Lanzhou University, and Mr. Shi Ze, a senior fellow at CIIS. Long-standing contacts with Dr. Dong Xiaoyang and Dr. Sun Zhuangzhi at China's Academy of Social Sciences (CASS) in Beijing gave the symposium access to their expertise. Finally, the compilation of this volume would not have been possible without the excellent translation work of Mr. Zhang (Tiger) Zhexin, a professor of English at Heilongjiang University in Harbin, and a Ph.D. student at Fudan University in Shanghai.

U.S. special recognition is accorded to the able services of panel moderators Mr. William O'Malley, Dr. Richard Giragosian, and Mr. Les Grau. Captain Randal Quan (USAF) of U.S. Pacific Command (PACOM) helped modify travel arrangements for Chinese scholars, offered Chinese language support, and assisted with several administrative details. Professor James Wirtz of NPS helped behind the scenes to arrange for BG Khan's keynote speech and one of his students, Mr. Colin Lober, assisted with a variety of issues, to include arranging a local tour of Monterey. Major Nicholas Reisdorff, an assistant Army attaché at the U.S. Embassy in Beijing, hosted dinner on the opening day of the symposium. Translators Professor Bao Chuanyun and Dr. Ling Lau provided superb simultaneous translation services, enhanced by the excellent audio technical services of Mr. John Bevan. Ms. Anna Donnelly of TRADOC was instrumental in assisting with funding issues; Ms. Erica Nelson of the Hilton Hotel ensured that all local administrative details were put in order; Mr. Robert Love of FMSO edited the final version of the proceedings; and Ms. Alice Mink of FMSO arranged flight itineraries, travel orders, and travel claims for all participants.

I wish to thank all of these people for their support and encouragement.

Mr. Charles Hawkins
Editor/Symposium Organizer

Chapter One

The New Great Game in Central Asia/South Asia: Continuity and Change

Feroz Hassan Khan

Introduction

In early June 2005 at the Shanghai Cooperation Organization's (SCO) foreign ministers meeting, India, Pakistan, and Iran were recommended for SCO "observer" status. Final SCO approval for the three countries will be considered at the next SCO heads of state meeting to be held on July 5-6, 2005 in Astana, Kazakhstan.[1] This is a major step, which accommodates each of the SCO member states' interests and the position of the SCO to further support a multi-polar world. This paper seeks to specifically address what is driving India and Pakistan's interest in joining the SCO? In order to answer this question, one must have an understanding of the SCO and its members. The SCO is comprised of China, Russia, Kazakhstan, Kyrgyzstan, Tajikistan and Uzbekistan. During the SCO's evolution, other countries in the region including Mongolia, Iran, India, Pakistan, and more recently the post-Taliban Afghan government, have expressed interest, to varying degrees, in participating in this emerging regional forum.[2]

The SCO is an emerging regional organization in Central Asia, but during its short history it has largely remained an enigma. It has been characterized as a security organization, a regional forum, and an anti-terrorism coalition. Another common characterization of the SCO is as a Russian- and Chinese-led alliance created to counter

---

[1] For coverage see: Valery Agarkov and Oral Karpishev, "Russian Spokesman: India, Iran, Pakistan To Join SCO as Observers," *Moscow ITAR-TASS* in English, 4 June 2005, FBIS Document ID: CEP20050604029012; "China Supports Pakistan, Iran, India Becoming SCO Observers," *Beijing Xinhua* in English, 7 June 2005, FBIS Document ID: CPP20050607000132; and "Transcript of PRC FM Spokesman News Conference on 7 Jun 05," *Beijing Ministry of Foreign Affairs of the People's Republic of China* WWW-Text in Chinese, 7 June 2005, FBIS Document ID: CPP20050607000171.

[2] As of the 2004 SCO meeting, only Mongolia has been granted "official observer" status, while Pakistan and Iran had later officially requested "observer" status. Pakistan and Iran's application status may be may be realized at the July 2005 SCO meeting in Astana, Kazakhstan. See Valery Agarkov, "Pakistan, Iran Apply for Observer Status in SCO," *Moscow ITAR-TASS* in English, 25 Feb 2005, FBIS Document ID: CEP20050225000340.

U.S. hegemony. These explanations of the SCO have their shortfalls and provide little insight into the primary motivations and interests driving the SCO's evolution. While analysis of this larger question is important, this paper seeks to examine the possibilities and implications of India, Pakistan or both joining the SCO as a full-fledged member. In order to answer this paper's research question, it is also important to understand the current geopolitical and geoeconomic relations between Central and South Asia. What bilateral relations currently exist between India/Pakistan and Russia, China, and the Central Asian states (Kazakhstan, Kyrgyzstan, Tajikistan, and Uzbekistan)? What barriers or tensions may bar future full membership? Is India more likely to be offered entry over Pakistan or vice versa? Which SCO member states support or oppose India or Pakistan's future membership and why? Finally, what do the answers to these questions tell us about the nature of the SCO itself? Is the SCO an alliance? Is it a regional economic forum? Or is it a modern day "concert" of Central Asia?

The Security Environment

Central and South Asia were historically linked through politics, culture and trade. Despite geographical hurdles interaction continued until these links were broken off when the Khanates of Bukhara and Khiva came under Russian control during the mid-nineteenth century. Since the collapse of the Soviet Union in 1991, changes to the regional political map have once again led to speculation as to whether past historical ties will be revived and how far old patterns of relations will be restored. The current security environment in Central Asia presents both challenges and opportunities for India and Pakistan to influence regional affairs.[3] India and Pakistan tend to balance one another in their regional economic and security policies. However, one's failure does not necessarily equate to future predictions of the others' success.

---

[3] Dianne L. Smith, *Central Asia: A New Great Game?* (Washington D.C.: Strategic Studies Institute, U.S. Army War College, 1996), 15.

According to Juli A. MacDonald, "India and Pakistan squandered opportunities to develop closer relations with the new Central Asian states in the early 1990s."[4] In the months leading up to September 11, 2001, both countries adjusted to fundamental changes in their strategic environment. India and Pakistan recognized that Central Asia was to play a critical role in their foreign policy calculations. India and Pakistan faced similar challenges regarding development of their regional policies in Central Asia. First, there are peer competitors in the region. Indian political elites have increasingly referred to Central Asia as part of "their 'extended strategic neighborhood' and as a region with which they share a range of strategic interests,"[5] while Pakistani political elites view Central Asia as "important because it gives Pakistan what they refer to as 'strategic depth'."[6] Second, Central Asia is viewed "as an arena that is critical to larger geopolitical competitions and realignments" in the post-Cold War environment.[7] For India this aspect is based on perceived threats, whether from Chinese encirclement or regional instability generated by the Afghan Taliban government. India also views the potential lack of access to a new east-west economic corridor—replacing the Cold War north-south orientation—as troubling. Finally, Central Asia represents an area for potential coöperation and conflict with the U.S. over state interests (e.g., countering Chinese influence or energy development and transportation routes). A third aspect of India and Pakistan's thinking toward Central Asia concerns non-energy related economic interests and increased trade relations.[8] Finally, MacDonald contends that energy resources (e.g. oil, gas, and hydropower) and pipeline politics will be a major driving force in relations between Central and South Asia.[9]

India

---

[4] Juli A. MacDonald, "South Asia" in *Central Asia and the South Caucasus: Reorientations, Internal Transitions, and Strategic Dynamics*," October 2002. Available from *Columbia International Affairs Online* <http://www.ciaonet.org/wps/dod122/index.html> (accessed 23 May 2005).

[5] Ibid.

[6] Ibid.

[7] Ibid.

[8] For India this involves IT, pharmaceuticals and hotels. For Pakistan this represents its goals under the auspicious of the ECO, by reducing trade barriers and offering the landlocked Central Asian states a viable means to the Arabian Sea.

[9] MacDonald, "South Asia."

India's "interest in the Central Asia region comes from a mixture of politico-strategic concerns and, perhaps to a lesser extent, perceived commercial prospects."[10] India's initial reaction to the newly independent states of Central Asia, was like China's, largely defensive in nature. The rapid growth of Pakistan, Iran and Turkey's influence in Central Asia generated a growing "concern and resentment in Indian nationalist circles."[11] The Indian political elites saw Pakistan's rapid rapprochement in Central Asia as an attempt to establish a bloc of Islam states.[12] Anthony Hyman argues that some Indian political elites interpreted the independence of the Central Asian states "in an alarmist fashion, as a highly unwelcome strengthening of Pakistan's regional position, with five potential new allies."[13] Of particular note were the reports claiming Pakistan had acquired enriched uranium from Tajikistan and Kazakhstan, while India's own efforts to acquire the same material from Kyrgyzstan, under International Atomic Energy Agency (IAEA) safeguards, had languished.[14] However, Indian nationalists, media discussions and reporting, largely overplayed fear of a new Muslim fundamentalist belt.

In time, "India's government took a more sanguine view" toward the Central Asia regimes. It came to an understanding "that none of the republics wanted the Islamic factor to count in their foreign relations, and that India quite as much as Pakistan could keep or gain further influence with these essentially secular-minded governments."[15] Anita Inder Singh argues that India's positive reengagement with the Central Asian states emerged due to new international and geopolitical realities. For Singh, India's attempts to establish "good relations with them is a matter of pragmatism as India's neighbors and rivals, Pakistan and China, are interested in the region."[16] India was able to capitalize on its past ties with the Soviet Union to press its advantage in Central Asia. India's prestige

---

[10] Anthony Hyman, "Central Asia's Relations with Afghanistan and South Asia," in *The New States of Central Asia and their Neighbors*, ed. Peter Ferdinand (London: Royal Institute of International Affairs, 1994), 81.

[11] Ibid., 85.

[12] Ross H. Munro, "Security Implications of the Competition for Influence Among Neighboring States: China, India, and Central Asia," in *After Empire: The Emerging Geopolitics of Central Asia*, ed. Jed C. Snyder (Washington D.C.: National Defense University Press, 1999), 132.

[13] Hyman, "Central Asia's Relations with Afghanistan and South Asia," 81.

[14] Ibid., 85.

[15] Ibid., 81-82.

[16] Anita Inder Singh, "India's Relations with Russia and Central Asia," *International Affairs* 71, no. 1 (January 1995), 78.

can largely be attributed to its culture, general goodwill and "as an old and trusted friend the Soviet era."[17]

Today, India is turning to the SCO not for security purposes but for economic motivations. India's interest in Central Asia and the SCO, by and large, is the result of its existing bilateral economic agenda. According to Singh, "India regards economic cooperation as the best way to counter Pakistan's influence in Central Asia."[18] The lynchpins of India's Central Asian regional economic policies have been Kazakhstan and Uzbekistan.

During the 1990s, "the actual volume of Indian trade with Central Asia remained modest."[19] India was able to secure both economic and security agreements with Uzbekistan.[20] India was also able to increase cooperation with Kazakhstan in the areas of technology exchanges and participation in space programs associated with the Baikonur cosmodrome.[21] India also offered $5 million in trade credits to both Kyrgyzstan and Turkmenistan. Finally, India increased cooperation with Tajikistan despite its internal instability. However, it was set back in its attempts to open an embassy in Dushanbe.

---

[17] Hyman, "Central Asia's Relations with Afghanistan and South Asia," 82. Hyman contends that the key to Indian prestige in the region derives not from "politics, fine arts, nor historical links, but instead from mass culture, in the form of the immensely popular Hindi film industry centered on Bombay, and the pop songs it spawns."[55]

[18] Singh, "India's relations with Russia and Central Asia," 79.

[19] Hyman, "Central Asia's Relations with Afghanistan and South Asia," 83. The most significant trade agreement from this period was a $75M deal signed between India and Uzbekistan in January 1992. Also see: FBIS 1/31/99-2/3/92

[20] The 1992 India-Uzbekistan treaty 'on the principles of interstate relations and bilateral cooperation' was similar to the 1993 India-Russian treaty. While neither treaty referenced direct military cooperation, they did have similar language concerning cooperation in fighting against terrorism, arms and drug trafficking and extremism. This language is similar to later documents associated with the SCO members' goals for the organization. See: Atul Aneja "Daily: India, Uzbekistan Holding Talks to Counter Terrorism," *Chennai The Hindu* in English, 27 April 2000, p. 13, FBIS Document ID: SAP20000427000066; Atul Aneja, "India Uzbekistan Sign Treaties To Fight Terrorism," *Chennai The Hindu* in English, 3 May 2000, p 13, FBIS Document ID: SAP20000503000033; "Indo-Uzbek Relations," Varanasi Aj in Hindi, 4 May 2000, p 6, FBIS Document ID: SAP20000509000033; "Uzbek President on Ties With India," *Tashkent Uzbek Television First Channel* in Russian, 4 May 2000, FBIS Document ID: CEP20000505000218; "Indian Foreign Minister Visits Uzbek Aviation Plant," *Tashkent Uzbekistan Television First Channel* in Russian, 19 May 1999, FBIS Document ID: FTS19990519001882; "India's Singh Holds Wide-Ranging Talks With Uzbek Leaders," *Calcutta The Telegraph* in English 19 May 1999, p 5, FBIS Document ID: FTS19990520000643; "Defense Ties With Uzbekistan," *Chennai The Hindu* in English 20 May 1999, p 10, FBIS Document ID: FTS19990521000609; and "Uzbekistan Seeks India's Help in Tackling Religious Extremism," *New Delhi Hindustan Times* (Internet Version-WWW) in English, 17 July 2000, FBIS Document ID: SAP20000717000026.

[21] On February 24, 1992, India began expressing interests in space cooperation with Kazakhstan's Baikonur cosmodrome, just as the cash-strapped Russian government was mothballing its Buran space shuttle.

Overall India was received well by the newly independent Central Asia states but retuned home with little to show for their efforts. A major constraint on India's efforts was that it had little funds to back up the goodwill visits. The "cash-strapped Indian Government, its budget vetted by the International Monetary Fund, could offer only training programs and, in some cases, trade credits."[22] Despite these government limitations, "Indian private companies were reportedly looking closely at Tajikistan's investment potential in silver, pharmaceuticals, coal, granite and leather goods for joint ventures."[23]

Despite its good standing and strong bilateral relationship with Russia, Ross H. Munro contends, "[i]n the final analysis, it was the overall weakness of India's economy, and not just the budgetary straits the New Delhi government was in, that limited India's ability to make an impact on the new republics."[24] China was able to displace India by "offering cheaper and better quality consumer goods, including Hong Kong-designed and Chinese-made garments, to the five republics."[25] A position China still maintains today.[26] By 1992, India's economic ambitions were stymied, and its political elites became less concerned about the region.

Pakistan

Pakistan's ambitions to form an Islamic bloc failed to materialize.[27] During the 1990s, Pakistan targeted the Central Asian states for better relations, but it did not yield the results initially sought. Pakistani political elites' visions of forming "a Muslim security belt stretching from Turkey to Pakistan with Central Asia as the 'buckle,' to provide both 'strategic depth' and needed allies in her policy struggles over Afghanistan and Kashmir," were quickly dashed.[28] Pakistan's support for the Taliban is a lingering source of friction between the Central Asian states. Fear of a spillover into the Tajik civil

---

[22] Munro, "Security Implications of the Competition for Influence Among Neighboring States: China, India, and Central Asia," 132.

[23] Anthony Hyman, "Central Asia's Relations with Afghanistan and South Asia," 85.

[24] Munro, "Security Implications of the Competition for Influence Among Neighboring States: China, India, and Central Asia," 132.

[25] Ibid., 132-133.

[26] India's latest recourse is to offer information technology exchanges for further cooperation.

[27] Munro, "Security Implications of the Competition for Influence Among Neighboring States: China, India, and Central Asia," 133.

[28] Smith, *Central Asia: A New Great Game?* 12.

war and Taliban support from the IMU in Uzbekistan, only further isolated Pakistan from Central Asia.[29] In addition, the Central Asia states reestablished their ties with Russia as their main security partner in the region through the May 1992 CIS collective security agreement. During the 1990's, Pakistan was forced to shift its focus in Central Asia to establishing bilateral economic and cultural ties and offering assistance on regional issues, such as counter-narcotics.

Pakistan's initial forays into Central Asia emphasized the economic dimension of its foreign policy goals. The primary bilateral mechanism used by Pakistan was the Economic Cooperation Organization (ECO),[30] which sought to create a common market for goods and services, as well as to develop capital and financial markets between Muslim countries.[31] Pakistan wanted access to Central Asia's energy resources and natural materials while offering to export textiles, machinery and telecommunications equipment. The process was started with high-level delegation visits to Central Asia between November-December 1991. The result was $30 million in credit offers tendered to Kazakhstan, Kyrgyzstan, and Tajikistan "to establish joint ventures in cotton, textiles, garments, pharmaceuticals, engineering goods, surgical instruments, telecommunications and agro-industry."[32] In the summer of 1992, Pakistan was also able to seal agreements with Uzbekistan "for the establishment of a satellite communications link, construction of highways, joint production of telecommunications equipment and the manufacture in Pakistan of rolling stock for Central Asian Railways."[33]

According to Dianne L. Smith, "Pakistan has had mixed success in bringing these bilateral agreements to fruition. They reflect the gap between intent and capability."[34] Smith attributes these constraints to a lack of direct geographic access to the region,

---

[29] See Melissa Iqbal and Teresita C. Schaffer, "Pakistan, the Middle East and Central Asia," *The South Asia Monitor* no. 30 (1 February 2001). Available from *The Center for Strategic and International Studies* <http://www.ciaonet.org> (accessed 24 April 2005).

[30] The ECO was established in 1985 as a successor to the 1964 Regional Cooperation for Development (RCD) consisting of Iran, Pakistan and Turkey. For Russian reactions to the ECO, see: Vyacheslav Ya. Belokrenitskiy, "Russia and greater Central Asia," *Asian Survey* 34, no. 12 (December 1994): 1093-1108. Available from *JSTOR* <http://www.jstor.org/> (accessed 24 April 2005).

[31] Tahir Amin, Pakistan, Afghanistan and the Central Asian States," in *The New Geopolitics of Central Asia and its Borderlands* , eds. Ali Banuazizi and Myron Weiner (Bloomington, Indiana: Indiana University Press, 1994), 221.

[32] Ibid.

[33] Ibid., 222.

[34] Smith, *Central Asia: A New Great Game?* 14.

regional instability, Pakistan's LOC infrastructure, and its lack of financial resources.[35] The final blow to Pakistan's early economic aspirations in Central Asia was the establishment of the Shanghai Five in 1996, followed by the creation of the SCO in 2001.

21st Century Foreign Policies and Strategic Incentives toward Central Asia and the SCO

The SCO has severely limited Pakistan's aspirations in Central Asia. The SCO has curtailed Pakistan's attempts at establishing "strategic depth" by seeking new Islamic allies in a collective security arrangement. The SCO also has offered regional non-Islamic powers that are in a more favorable geographic position, such as Russia and China, the opportunity to exploit the regions' energy resources. Joining the SCO may offer Pakistan the best channel to revisit its 1990s objectives and goals in Central Asia.

India's "Look East" foreign policy orientation seeks to enhance economic and military ties with countries in Southeast Asia. While its "Look West" policy, which is directed toward the Middle East and Central Asia, has not yet developed into a coherent strategy. India's demand for energy resources is largely driven by three factors: the rapid growth of its economy; the status of its domestic energy sector; and its attempts at diversifying its oil and gas imports.[36] If India is serious about increasing its access to energy resources in Central Asia and the Middle East, it will have to come to a political arrangement with Pakistan.[37] However, this foreign policy track of economic interdependence may compete with India's future regional goals and lingering security concerns.

---

[35] Ibid.

[36] For energy cooperation and competition in Central Asia, see: Ibragim Alibekov, "India Set to Expand Presence in Central Asia," 3 December 2003, Available from *Eurasianet.Org* <http://www.eurasianet.org/departments/business/articles/eav120303.shtml> (Accessed 23 May 2005); and Nikola Krastev, "Central Asia: Strapped for Energy Resources, China and India Look for Alternatives," 22 April 2004. Available from *Radio Free Europe/Radio Liberty* <http://www.rferl.org/featuresarticle/2004/4/E62756BE-A943-41F1-B03E-86D920CB1188.html> (Accessed 23 May 2005).

[37] For an analysis of how India and Pakistan can increase cooperation in the energy sector, see: C. Raja Mohan, "Indian Analyst Emphasized Need for 'Larger' Vision of 'Look West' Policy, *Chennai The Hindu (Internet Version-WWW)* in English, 17 June 2004, FBIS Document ID: SAP20040617000014.

India's 21st century ambition to be a global power has one major consequence. Its aspiration to "rise to a global status would be to leave Pakistan trailing behind as a minor regional power that could no longer threaten India's vital interests."[38] Joining the SCO would build on India's existing bilateral economic and military ties with the Central Asian states and Russia. Improving military logistics with Iran, Tajikistan,[39] Kazakhstan, Kyrgyzstan[40] and Uzbekistan[41] is critical to India's strategic vision. Joining the SCO may also make establishing a permanent, stable relationship with China more likely.[42] However, the events of September 11, 2001 may impact India's long-term regional calculus.[43]

---

[38] Stephen Blank, "India's Grand Strategic Vision Gets Grander," *Asia Times* (25 December 2003). Available from *Asian Times Online* <http://www.atimes.com/atimes/South_Asia/EL25Df09.html> (accessed 23 May 2005). Also see Stephen Blank, "India's Continuing Drive into Central Asia," *Central Asia and Caucasus Analyst* (14 January 2004): 8-9. Available from *The Central Asia Caucasus Institute* <http://www.cacianalyst.org/issues/20040114Analyst.pdf> (accessed 13 June 2005).

[39] For details of India's military engagement in Tajikistan, especially information regarding the Farkhor/Ayni airbase and plans to conduct joint exercises, see: Saikat Datta, "India Gets Military Partner in Central Asia," *New Delhi The Indian Express (Internet Version-WWW)* in English, 13 February 2003. FBIS Document ID: SAP20030213000018; P. Jayaram, "India Sets Up Military Base in Tajikistan," *New Delhi Hindustan Times (Internet Version-WWW)* in English, 16 August 2002, FBIS Document ID: SAP20020816000045; "Indian Defense Ministry Denies Military Base Set Up on Tajik-Afghan Border," *New Delhi Hindustan Times (Internet Version-WWW)* in English, 16 August 2002, FBIS Document ID: *SAP20020816000099;* and Justin Burke, "Russia, China, India stress good ties with Tajikistan," (Jan 05 2004). Available from *Eurasian.Org,* <http://www.eurasianet.org/resource/tajikistan/hypermail/200401/0000.shtml > (accessed 25 April 2005).

[40] For details see: Justin Burke, "Visiting Kyrgyz president vows to boost cooperation with India," (Nov 11 2003). Available from *Eurasian.Org,* <http://www.eurasianet.org/resource/kyrgyzstan/hypermail/200311/0017.shtml> (accessed 25 April 2005).

[41] For details on India's military interests in Uzbekistan and Kazakhstan, see the following: Sudha Ramachandran, "India Revels in New Diplomatic Offensive," Asian Times (22 November 2003). Accessed from *Asian Times Online* <http://www.atimes.com/atimes/South_Asia/EK22Df05.html> (accessed 23 May 2005); "Uzbekistan's Aviation Industry Booms," *BBC News*, (18 December 2001). Accessed from *BCC Online* <http://news.bbc.co.uk/1/hi/business/1716939.stm> (accessed 23 May 2005); and K. R. Jawahar, "India and Kazakhstan," *SAPRA Articles and Factsheets*, (24 February 2002). Available from *SAPRA* <http://www.subcontinent.com/sapra/research/centralasia/articles/ca_article_20020224a_html.html> (accessed 23 May 2005).

[42] For the prospects of Chinese-Indian cooperation and competition, see: Tshering Chonzom, "China-India Relations in a Regional Perspective," *New Delhi Institute of Peace and Conflict Studies* WWW-Text in English 11 December 2004, FBIS Document ID: SAP20041216000089.

[43] One former Indian officer provides a detailed analysis of why India should wait on the SCO and makes a good case for continuing bilateral relations with the SCO members and additionally focusing on Afghanistan instead of aggressively pursuing SCO membership. See Brig Arun Sahgal (Ret.), "India Should Re-evaluate its Desire to Join Shanghai Cooperation Organization," *New Delhi Force (Internet Version-WWW)* in English, 14 April 2005, FBIS Document ID: SAP20050414000053.

Post September 11th, India's diplomatic charge into Central Asia has largely been driven by its future energy requirements.[44] Strategic repositioning also weighs in India's security calculations since the Taliban government was ousted from Afghanistan.[45] According to Rahul Bedi, the U.S.' continued presence in the Central Asian region and the Chinese-India nuclear rivalry are "also fueling New Delhi's 'forward' Central Asian policy."[46] Although "India remains powerless to engineer or overtly influence the 'New Game,' its size, military and nuclear capability make it a not altogether insignificant part of the complex jigsaw" puzzle.[47]

Russia fully supports India's entry into the SCO as a full fledged member. Russia and India share a "broad congruence on a whole range of strategic issues. But it is the defense and military-technical cooperation which is the lynchpin of the strategic partnership."[48] Kazakhstan's President Nazarbayev also has openly supported India's inclusion in the SCO, as well as its becoming a permanent member of the UN Security Council.[49] Nevertheless, India may be having second thoughts on joining the SCO with Russia and China as a "strategic triangle" promoting a multi-polar world. India's growing strategic partnership with the U.S. might "likely put Delhi in an awkward situation if it

---

[44] For general trends and demands of India's energy sector, see: "Economic Trends and Prospects in Developing Asia: South Asia," in *Asian Development Outlook 2004*. Available from *Asian Development Bank Website* <http://www.adb.org/Documents/Books/ADO/2004/ADO2004_PART2_SA.pdf#page=13,120> (accessed 23 May 2005): 120-125; "India Country Analysis Brief," October 2004. Available from *Energy Information Agency Online* <http://www.eia.doe.gov/emeu/cabs/india.html#back> (accessed 23 May 2005); and "India's Share from Foreign Oil Fields To Go Up," 30 October 2003. Available from *Rediff.com* <http://www.rediff.com/money/2003/oct/30oil.htm> (Accessed 23 May 2005). For broader coverage of Russian and Chinese military cooperation with India and Pakistan, see: Scott Baldauf, "Selling Arms to India and Pakistan: Explosive Business," *The Christian Science Monitor* 27 November 2002, 7. Available from *ProQuest* <http://proquest.umi.com/login> (accessed 24 April 2005).

[45] Sergei Blagov, "Russia Seeking to Strengthen Regional Organizations to Counterbalance Western Influence," 04 December 2002. Available from *Eurasian.Org* <http://www.eurasianet.org/departments/insight/articles/eav120402a_pr.shtml> (accessed 25 April 2005).

[46] Rahul Bedi, "India and Central Asia," *Frontline* 19 no. 19, (14-27 September 2002). Available from *Frontline* <http://www.flonnet.com/fl1919/19190600.htm> (accessed 23 May.2005).

[47] Ibid.

[48] Ashok K. Mehta, "India-Russia: Life after Defense," *New Delhi The Pioneer (Internet Version-WWW)* in English, 04 December 2002, FBIS Document ID: *SAP20021204000068*. For more on Russia-India ties, see: J.N. Dixit, "Vajpayee in Russia and Central Asia: Meaningful Revival of Equations," 17 November 2003. Available from *Indian News Online* <http://news.indiamart.com/news-analysis/vajpayee-in-russia-a-432.html> (Accessed 23 May 2005).

[49] See "Kazakhstan shares India's concerns on terrorism," *Mumbai The Times of India (Internet Version-WWW)* in English, 13 February 2002, FBIS Document ID: SAP20020213000031.

did indeed join the SCO, given the organization's revised, albeit unstated, charter of containing Washington's burgeoning influence in the region."[50] New Delhi is also extremely cautious about joining any security forum, especially with China as a leading player, especially if China's military and nuclear partner Pakistan is also a likely member.[51] A senior Indian diplomat commented that until "SCO membership rules are finalized we cannot assess whether joining it will be advantageous or not for India."[52] The officials further indicated "that the key to India's relations with the Central Asian Region depended largely on China's response to the U.S. military presence in the region."[53]

Post September 11th, Pakistan has found a new ally in Central Asia and a strong supporter for its membership in the SCO. Uzbekistan seems ready to move past the Pakistani government's former support for radical Islamic groups in Central Asia.[54] Security issues and increased bilateral economic cooperation were on the agenda during a recent meeting in Tashkent. Presidents Islom Karimov and Pervez Musharraf both see a common threat from extremism, terrorism, organized crime and narcotics trafficking. Both leaders want to destroy the root causes of terrorism. Economically, Uzbekistan is interested in gaining accesses to Pakistan's major Indian Ocean ports of Karachi and Gwadar. Despite this latest goodwill, the specter of Islamic radicals who fled Uzbekistan and sought refuge in Pakistan remains a "delicate issue."[55] One may speculate as to

---

[50] Bedi, "India and Central Asia."

[51] For more Indian commentary on the merits for a proposed Russia-China-India alliance, see: "Triangular Cooperation," *Chennai Dinamani* in Tamil, 04 December 2002; FBIS Document ID: SAP20021205000032; "The Russians are here," *New Delhi The Indian Express (Internet Version-WWW)* in English 04 December 2002; FBIS Document ID: SAP20021204000026; and Jasjit Singh, "Putin the right perspective," *New Delhi The Indian Express (Internet Version-WWW)* in English, 04 December 2002, FBIS Document ID: SAP20021204000012

[52] Rahul Bedi, "India and Central Asia."

[53] Ibid.

[54] For press coverage of Presidents Islom Karimov and Pervez Musharraf's news conference and details of areas for increased cooperation on security issues and economic ties, see: "Uzbekistani, Pakistani Presidents Discuss Counterterrorism Cooperation," *Tashkent Uzbek Television First Channel* in Uzbek, 06 Mar 2005, FBIS Document ID: CEP20050307000151.; "Pakistan's Musharraf Meets Uzbekistan's Karimov, Sign Anti-Terror Agreement," *Tashkent Uzbek Radio 1* in Uzbek 06 Mar 2005, FBIS Document ID: CEP20050307000011.; and "FYI -- Musharraf Says Pakistan, Uzbekistan To Cooperate Against Terrorist Groups," *Tashkent Uzbek Television First Channel* in Uzbek 06 Mar 05, FBIS Document ID: CEP20050306000079.

[55] President Karimov cited in "Uzbekistani, Pakistani Presidents Discuss Counterterrorism Cooperation," *Tashkent Uzbek Television First Channel* in Uzbek 06 Mar 05, FBIS Document ID: CEP20050307000151.

whether a new regional North-South axis is forming between Uzbekistan, Afghanistan, and Pakistan, all strong political and military allies of the U.S.' Global War on Terrorism. If this is the case, Pakistan's bid to become a member of the SCO may have strong implications on the overall SCO orientation, potentially creating a pro-U.S. support bloc. In this case, the Indian elites which have historically suspected an U.S.-Pakistan-China strategic triangle aimed at limiting India's rise to a great power status might well pursue a counter policy by establishing an India-Iran-Tajikistan triangle. Regardless of myth or fact, one should expect a continued game of "one-upmanship" as India and Pakistan seek greater security and economic ties in Central Asia.

Part I

A Framework of Understanding

Chapter Two

China's Central Asia Policy

Zhao Huasheng

China's View on the Situation in Central Asia

China and Central Asian states share the same borders, similar cultures, and a long history of communication. China must pay close attention to Central Asia, where it has important national interests.

Since their independence, due to their special geopolitical position and various problems during the transformation period, Central Asian states have been a victim of growing international terrorism, national separatism and religious extremism, as well as smuggling, drug dealing and arms dealing, which also pose serious threats to the surrounding nations including China:

Most Central Asian states are confronted with grave domestic problems, such as the fragile political structure, serious internal conflicts, poverty, and huge social gaps. For example, the civil war lasted nearly five years in Kazakhstan, a country with a population of only 5 million, since its independence, which brought about great losses and trauma in the country. Although Central Asian states are on their way to stability, unstable factors still exist. China expects to see the long-term peace and stability, rather than political turbulence, in Central Asia.

Despite the long historical connections in politics, economy, nationalities, religion, society and culture, Central Asian states are facing various conflicts in nationalities, religion, territory, and natural resources, etc., which often cause discord and clashes among these states. For example, Ferghana, the small yet densely-populated basin, belongs to Uzbekistan, Kyrgyzstan and Tajikistan, with indefinite borders between them, as well as mixed population of Uzbeks, Tajiks and Kyrgyzs, which has already brought about many nationality clashes in history. China hopes that all the Central Asian states are friendly to each other and solve their problems by negotiation, instead of hostility or even force.

Although the economy of Central Asian states is becoming more stable since 1995 and has begun to recover since the late 1990s, it still faces many difficult problems such as unemployment, poverty and widening social gaps, which may not only lead to political instability and social turmoil, but also help foster the "three forces" of smuggling, drug- and arms-trafficking. Meanwhile, China-Central Asia economic cooperation can hardly proceed without the steady growth of the Central Asian economy. Therefore, China expects the development and prosperity of the Central Asian economy, which will provide a favorable environment for their economic cooperation.

Under the post-Cold-War geopolitical milieu, not only is the strategic position of Central Asia noticeable again, but the region is also considered as a major base for energy in the 21st century. Thus, many large powers have begun to engage themselves in the region, competing with each other for more interests: the U.S. began its engagement through NATO's Partnership for Peace, as well as financial aid and investment, and set up military bases after 9/11, while Russia maintains its traditional influence over the region. As a neighbor of Central Asia, China hopes it does not turn out to be a battlefield for competition among great powers that may add to its instability.

Despite the improvement in the political and economic situations in the region, the development of Central Asia is still quite uncertain in many respects, such as the precarious foundation of state power, serious economic problems, the widening gap between the rich and the poor, complicated social problems, as well as the powerful religious forces that lead to political and social rupture. Moreover, in the complicated surrounding environment, Central Asia is troubled by the "three forces" of smuggling, as well as drug and arms dealing; there are also many disputes among Central Asian states on such issues as religion, politics, water, and other resources, etc. The intervention of the large powers has also further complicated the situation in the region. The political conflicts caused by the congressional election in Kyrgyzstan in March 2005 and the turmoil in Anjijon, Uzbekistan in May both indicate the possibility of further turbulence in Central Asia. Due to such uncertainties, the development of the region, as well as its future policies, is also hard to predict.

Current Status of China's Engagement in Central Asia

Since the independence of the Central Asian states, China's influence over the region has remained very strong, and this is easy to understand. One reason is geographical proximity: China shares the same borders of over 3,000 kilometers with Kazakhstan, Kyrgyzstan and Tajikistan, and is very close to Uzbekistan and Turkmenistan. In fact, China is the country closest to Central Asia, as well as the one that borders the most Central Asian states. Another important issue between China and the Central Asian states is border definition. Negotiations on border issues were in progress between China and the Soviet Union when the Central Asian states obtained their independence. After the disintegration of the Soviet Union, most of its western borders with China become borders between China and three Central Asian states that decided to stand on Russia's side to continue negotiations with China. Even after the resolution of border disputes, the common pursuit of border security keeps joining China and Central Asia together. A third reason is the connections between the minority nationalities in northwest China and Central Asia in ethnic groups, religion, culture, history and tradition. Finally, the rich legacy of long historical connections in the region, though concealed over the past one and a half centuries, has resumed its effect in China-Central Asia relations. For the above-mentioned four reasons, China has been a country with great influence over Central Asia since its independence from the Soviet Union.

Central Asian states are less developed than most other former Soviet states. The disintegration of the Soviet Union witnessed the collapse of the planned economy and universal economic recession, while the Central Asian states suffered even more due to their poor economic foundations. Under these circumstances, cheap but durable Chinese goods poured into the region as the main source of daily commodities for the residents with low purchasing power. Therefore, the development of border trade is another means for China's engagement in Central Asia.

With the Taliban's seizure of state power in Afghanistan in the mid-1990s, Central Asia, Russia and China were all subjected to the threats of terrorism, separatism and extremism to different degrees. For further cooperation and attacking terrorism, The "Shanghai Five-State Organization" was founded in 1996 by China, Russia and three Central Asian states after their border negotiations, and is not only an important mechanism for China to safeguard its own security, but also the major means for China's engagement in Central Asian security affairs. In 2001, the "Shanghai 5-State Organization" became "Shanghai Cooperation Organization," or SCO, a mechanism for regional cooperation, which marks a breakthrough in China's diplomacy in Central Asia. The significance of the SCO to China is that it provides China with a security safeguarding mechanism and an institutionalized means for China's engagement in Central Asian affairs, as well as a platform for overall cooperation between China and Central Asian states. The establishment of the SCO also indicates that China and Russia have compromised with each other and reached a strategic balance in Central Asia, as well as acknowledged each other's interests in the region. In contrast, most Western media tend to take SCO as the joint attempt of China and Russia to prevent the U.S. and NATO from entering Central Asia. Generally speaking, through SCO, China has begun to demonstrate its strong position and potential in Central Asia.

After 9/11, the U.S. military force entered Central Asia, resulting in the collapse of the Taliban regime and great changes in the security situation and geopolitics of Central Asia, especially seen from the unexpected cooperation between Russia and the U.S., the pro-American tendency of Central Asian states in politics, and the growing U.S. influence in Central Asia, all of which affect China's position in the region. Many analysts think that 9/11 diminished the importance of the SCO in the security guarantee system of Central Asia and constrained the development of China's engagement in the region. Although Central Asia's post-9/11 geopolitical situation is unfavorable to China in some sense, its impact on China is not as strong as many foreign media believe it to be, and China's assessment of its own situation is not as pessimistic either. The major reason for this gap of perceptions is that foreign media tend to observe China-U.S. relations from geopolitical perspectives, emphasizing their competition and opposition, whereas China does not take the U.S. as a natural competitor or enemy, or take every U.S.-China encounter as confrontation; besides, foreign media may have misperceived China's strategic goals in Central Asia as aiming to control the region. As a matter of fact, because China has never attempted to control Central Asia, its strategic position in Central Asia is not as seriously frustrated as reported by most Western media; the China-Russia relationship is not much changed with the improvement in Russia-U.S. relations, while the relationship between China and Central Asian states is not obviously impaired either; the SCO has also survived the change, rather than collapsing as many analysts predicted. Hence, in spite of the new challenges China must face in the post-9/11 geopolitical situation in Central Asia, its strategic position in the region is not seriously weakened.

Foundation for China's Engagement in Central Asia

Two major means, multilateral and bilateral, are adopted to develop China-Central Asia relations. The SCO, the major multilateral means at present, serves as a solid platform for the development of China-Central Asia relations; it provides an institutionalized framework that engages China in the political, economic and security process of Central Asia, so that all can pursue their common interests. The bilateral means—the bilateral relations between China and Central Asian states—has the same importance as, but is even more fundamental than, the multilateral means. Given their respective functions and features, both means should be adopted to complement each other for the best implementation of China's Central Asia policy. As the Chinese saying goes, "we must walk with both legs." The SCO and the many bilateral relations, as they were, are the two legs with which China can stand firmly in Central Asia.

In fact, China enjoys many distinctive diplomatic resources in Central Asia. China's large size and its proximity to the Central Asian states are undoubtedly China's geopolitical advantages in the region, which naturally makes China one of the lasting and important factors in Central Asian issues. In addition, direct flight connections, together with many roads and railways, have increasingly facilitated the communication between people and goods across their borders.

For Central Asia, China is an irreplaceable partner in border security, as well as a guarantor of regional security. The security of the 3,000-km-long borders between China and three Central Asian states depends on their cooperation alone, where no other country can replace the position of China. Moreover, China is one of the safeguards for Central Asian security by means of bilateral cooperation and the SCO.

As a large nation and a balancing power among the major powers in Central Asia, China is crucial to the "balancing diplomacy" and "multi-directional diplomacy" of the

Central Asian states. In the meantime, China's diplomatic culture appeals very much to the Central Asian states: China does not seek hegemony or bully small states, neither does it intend to interfere in the domestic affairs of other countries; instead, it treats each Central Asian state equally and is willing to solve all problems through just negotiations. This "soft power" is playing an ever more important part in China's Central Asia policy.

Nonetheless, China's biggest advantage in Central Asia is its economy, which is not only China's greatest potential political and diplomatic resource, but also holds the greatest appeal to Central Asia. China has already become a massive economic entity, and its economy is expected to continue growing rapidly, which will exert more and more influence on the Central Asian economy and render China a closer economic partner with the region. It can be predicted for certain that China will become an important trading partner, investor, and financial-aid provider for Central Asia, as well as a large market for Central Asian energy and mineral products, and an important outlet for Central Asian transportation. However, we must also note that the growth of the influence of China's economy is ongoing and will not take place over night.

China also has many disadvantages in Central Asia: due to many years of separation between China and the Central Asian states, both have a quite limited understanding of each other, especially in Central Asia, where depictions of the old image of China still endure; current Chinese investment and economic activity are comparatively limited; China's political and social cultures do not appeal much to the young generation in Central Asia; besides, the long borders between both sides are likely to generate more disputes or conflicts while facilitating their communication.

Economic Relations between China and Central Asia

At present, there is no serious political problem between China and Central Asian states; their border disputes have been resolved and their cooperation on border security has been institutionalized; in addition, China maintains good relations with every Central Asian state. Therefore, their economic relations are the crucial factor that determines the further development of their relations. In other words, the further development of China-

Central Asia relations mainly depends on the enhancement of their economic cooperation.

Economic relations between both sides have developed rapidly over the past decade: the total trade volume between China and all four Central Asian states (Turkmenistan not included) in 1992 was only a little more than $500 million; it reached $2.3 billion in 2002, and $5 billion in 2004. Trade between both sides is also expected to increase at a faster rate in the coming years.

However, with the change in the trade environment, China faces new challenges. The major form of trade between both sides over the past decade has been of daily commodities, especially by people-to-people trade on a crude level. People-to-people trade—mainly buying and selling of low-end goods in big public markets—emerged under the specific circumstances at the time of the independence of Central Asian states, and played a crucial role in helping poor families to survive the hard times. Yet this form of trade cannot continue enhancing China-Central Asia economic cooperation any more, due to its growing limitations. On the one hand, with more restrictions from the government and the need for standardization, Chinese goods that enter the Central Asian market by this means will cost more, and thus lose their price advantage; on the other hand, with the gradual improvement of Central Asian economy, personal incomes will increase too, resulting in the decreased demand for low-end Chinese goods. For these two reasons, Chinese goods may have a smaller share in the Central Asian market for a certain period of time. As people-to-people trade is the major form of China's engagement in the market, a smaller share of the market will affect China's economic engagement in Central Asia on the whole. This tendency is similar to China's engagement in the Russian market, except that it develops more slowly than in Russia. China should take active measures to stop the tendency.

China's rapid economic growth has manifold meanings to Central Asian states. On the one hand, it is a good opportunity for them; on the other, however, because of the relatively weak economic foundation as well as less developed industry and technologies, they are afraid of being economically marginalized as only a supplier of raw materials for China. Indeed, China is not the cause for the weak industrial foundation and large proportion of raw-material industry in the economic structure of Central Asian states;

neither is China the only country that mainly needs Central Asian raw materials, as Western investment in the region is also centered on the fields of energy and raw materials. Nevertheless, this is still a big problem that China must face in developing its relations with Central Asian states.

Need for China's Readjustment of Its Economic Policy in Central Asia

In view of the current problems and the changing situation, China should readjust its economic policy in Central Asia in order to better conduct its economic cooperation with Central Asian states.

While developing people-to-people trade with Central Asian states, China should place more emphasis on other means of economic cooperation, especially investment and joint ventures, in order to further enhance China-Central Asia economic and political cooperation. In reality, such types of cooperation are more needed and welcome in Central Asian states, therefore, China should attend to their needs and interests in the cooperation for mutual benefit. Many difficulties exist in the development of bilateral cooperation between both sides in investment and joint venture: for China, there are obstacles in the management system and policies, and for Central Asia, the problem of the environment for investment. Due to the complicated environment at present, investment in Central Asia entails great risks. Moreover, China is not yet a big country in capital output. Nonetheless, with its rapid economic development and its overseas investment policy becoming more flexible, China is beginning to invest more in other countries. Thus, more Chinese investment in Central Asia can be expected in the future, with the amelioration of the environment for investment and management in the region. During past China-Central Asia economic cooperation, the government tended to supervise Chinese enterprises with administrative orders, which has proven unsuitable for the law of economy and the markets, and thus very inefficient. Except for large-scale joint ventures between states, the main function of the government should be guiding enterprises, providing them with information, consultation, recommendations and other necessary service, as well as helping them avoid risks.

In order to further enhance its economic cooperation with Central Asia, China should encourage the participation of more private capital, especially from the coastal provinces in the east and the south. With a more flexible and efficient capital mechanism, Chinese private enterprises are more adaptive to the transforming economic environment of Central Asia. Frontier provinces in China are the leading player in China-Central Asia economic cooperation, with their irreplaceable advantages in geography and culture, while the coastal provinces possess more capacities in science and technology, as well as investment. Thus, it is necessary to make more use of the technologies and capital in east China.

Another important task for China in its economic cooperation with Central Asia is to establish the reputation of Chinese products. The large amount of poor-quality Chinese products that entered the Commonwealth of Independent States (CIS) market in the early 1990s seriously damaged the reputation of Chinese products, a situation can only be remedied through strenuous efforts. Above all, it is necessary to distinguish the quality of a product from its grade: different products have different grades according to different costs and quality standards, yet low-grade products do not necessarily mean poor quality; as long as they pass a certain quality standard, they should be accepted for their price. At present, most Chinese products in the Central Asian market are low-end for the following reasons: 1) China is the leading country in the production of low-end products for the low costs of Chinese labor; 2) the Central Asian market has great demands for low-end products for its comparatively low purchasing power; and 3) it is easy for small businesses in China to join in the market for relatively easy access across the border. In general, Central Asian consumers tend to accept Chinese low-end products, instead of high-tech products, which have already had a certain share in the European and American markets for their good quality and advantage in price. Thus it can be said that the difficulty of Chinese high-tech products in the Central Asian market is mainly rooted in the bad image of Chinese products as a whole. In order to lift its economic cooperation with Central Asia to a new level, China should strive to create a new image for Chinese products and eliminate the negative effects of the old one.

Furthermore, China is also likely to encounter a new problem in bilateral relations, i.e., how to develop its relations with Kazakhstan and Uzbekistan respectively. China maintains the same policy regarding each Central Asian state, and tends to develop a friendly and cooperative relationship with each one while trying to keep an overall balance among them. Kazakhstan and Uzbekistan are two big states in Central Asia, both maintaining good relations with China. The current problem, however, is that the growth of common interests between China and Kazakhstan is much faster than between China and Uzbekistan; there is a tendency toward imbalance in the development their national relations.

Kazakhstan is not only the biggest neighbor state of China in Central Asia, with the longest common border and sharing the most ports with China, but there are also over one million of Kazaks living in Xinjiang, China. As a result, private communication between both countries is the easiest and most frequent, with the most active trade and closely intertwined interests. Yet from another perspective, such close communication also brings about more problems than between China and other states, such as immigration issues and disputes over water resources, among others.

Kazakhstan is of crucial importance to China, as most of China's interests in Central Asia are reflected in Kazakhstan: the first is in border security, because they share a common border of more than 1,700 kilometers, more than half of the total that China shares with Central Asia; the second is in anti-terrorism, for Kazakhstan is both the major stage for the "East Turkistan Movement" and the main passage for the connections of the Movement with international terrorist forces; the next is in their economic cooperation, since Kazakhstan is China's biggest partner for trade in Central Asia, with their trade volume in 2004 exceeding $4 billion, far ahead of that between China and other Central Asian states; lastly, Kazakhstan is the most important Central Asian partner in energy; an important breakthrough in their energy cooperation is very likely that China's oil imports from Kazakhstan may reach 10 million tons in the coming few years, which will substantially strengthen China's interests in Kazakhstan.

Uzbekistan is another large state in Central Asia that has also shared a good relationship with China. Yet unlike with Kazakhstan, common interests between China and Uzbekistan center on politics, regional security and anti-terrorism. On the one hand, the fact that there is no common border between both countries saves a lot of problems for them, such as disputes over water or border issues, and the responsibility for environmental pollution, etc; on the other hand, transportation between both countries is not convenient enough for their further cooperation. Their economic cooperation, for example, is developing comparatively slowly: in 2003, their total trade volume was only little more than $300 million, almost 1/10 of that between China and Kazakhstan. Moreover, despite the potential oil and natural gas reserves in Uzbekistan, there is not yet a large-scale joint program between both countries for energy exploitation. All the above-mentioned factors lead to a stark contrast between China-Kazakhstan relations and China-Uzbekistan relations, which may be even sharper once the China-Kazakhstan oil pipeline is constructed. At that time, Kazakhstan will hold a much more important position in China's diplomacy and economy, whereas Uzbekistan's position will become even less important, resulting in certain imbalance between China's relations with these two states.

How to maintain the relative balance between relations with Kazakhstan and Uzbekistan is a difficult task for Chinese diplomacy. While developing its relations with Kazakhstan, China needs to pay more efforts to its economic cooperation with Uzbekistan. To achieve this goal, railway and road transportation is of special significance. It is estimated that trade volume between both countries may easily double with the solution of the railway transportation problems. Meanwhile, China should identify the growth points and potential of its economic cooperation with Uzbekistan according to the characteristics of Uzbek economy.

Furthermore, China needs to enhance its economic cooperation with Kyrgyzstan and Tajikistan as well. In view of the fact that there are few oil and natural gas resources in the two countries, China should find out the fields in which their cooperation can be conducted. Because both Kyrgyzstan and Tajikistan are relatively small economic entities with no ambition to compete with Kazakhstan and Uzbekistan, China's relations with both states are less subject to the influence of external factors, thus remaining rather stable.

Chapter Three

The Security of Central Asia and Its Impact on China

Sun Zhuangzhi

With an area of about 4 million square kilometers and a total population of 56 million, Central Asia security is confronted with many serious threats and practical problems, which directly affects the stability and development of northwest China, especially Xinjiang, China.

Complexity of Central Asian Security

Although the original rule of security based on bipolar confrontation was shattered with the end of the Cold War, its remaining effect keeps troubling West Asia and South Asia, among other regions. The Palestine-Israel conflicts, India-Pakistan confrontation, as well as the civil war in Afghanistan, are doomed to last, while the disintegration of the Soviet Union facilitates the infiltration of external unstable factors, resulting in a "shattered security zone" in some frontier areas of the former Soviet Union. Central Asia lies right in the zone. Due to their limited power and rather weak national security system, as well as many difficulties in the political and economic development, the five Central Asian states are facing a rigid security situation.

Two factors are the key to the stability of the newly independent states, namely stability of the border and identity of residents of all nationalities with the new state, both extremely difficult to achieve for Central Asian states. According to Russian scholars, there are at least 19 disputed areas in Central Asia, which will bring about many conflicts in the future. There are also over 100 nationalities living in the region, and violent conflicts between some nationalities happened in the Soviet times; the emigration tide after the independence of Central Asian states indicates the lack of trust between them; many minority nationalities worry about, or are discontented with, the policies of the new states.

Nevertheless, real threats for Central Asian security are the nontraditional factors: many nontraditional security problems have plagued the region since the end of last century, terrorism as the most serious one; the Central Asian security environment is further complicated by such issues as extremism, drug dealing, arms smuggling, epidemics and ecological problems. Conspicuously, most of the problems are transnational, with universal harm to all Central Asian states.

Persistence of Transnational Crime

A crucial factor threatening Central Asian security is the problem of transnational drug and arms smuggling. The drug output in Afghanistan in 2002 reached 3,400 tons, 65 percent of which were transported across the Tajikistan-Afghanistan border, and then to Europe and Russia via Central Asia, but only 10 percent of the transportation can be intercepted by law-enforcing sectors of Central Asian states. Meanwhile, as the wild opium poppies in the region can be made into 30 tons of opium, Central Asia itself has become one of the four largest drug producing regions in the world, and is called "the Golden Crescent Zone" together with Afghanistan, Pakistan and Iran. The booming drug business leads to an increase of the number of drug addicts and drug-related crimes in the region.

Another important financial resource for local terrorist organizations is the smuggling of arms and military technologies. Besides, Central Asia is an important passage for the transportation of arms to Afghanistan. For example, Russian frontier forces have confiscated 1,500 illegal weapons on the Tajikistan-Afghanistan border since 1992.

The Expanding 'Three Forces'

In the political context in the late 1980s, extremist forces in Central Asia began to spread. First, due to the ideological confusion in the late years of the Soviet Union, they grew very fast in Central Asia, a region with many religious and ethnic problems; second, the political pluralism gave rise to many extremist organizations with political colors; next, extremist forces abroad took advantage of the occasion and began to infiltrate into Central Asia; lastly, the situation in Central Asia was once out of control at the time of the disintegration of the Soviet Union, so that extremist forces made a few attempts to seize the state power in Uzbekistan and Tajikistan, both with a long Islamic tradition. Taking the densely populated Ferghana Basin as their base, they attempted to spread to other areas.

The Tajik civil war broke out in March 1992. The scheme of the extremist forces, including the Islamic Restoration Party, to seize the state power by force, was opposed by most areas. Thus, they were soon expelled out of the capital, Dushanbe, and fled to the mountainous areas and the border areas of Afghanistan. In autumn 1993, the extremists of Tajikistan established a new religious party, the Islamic Restoration Movement (IRM), in Afghanistan, and in 1996, the Uzbekistan Islamic Movement (IMU). Apart from support it receives from international terrorist organizations, the IMU is also engaged in such crimes as drug smuggling and kidnapping, and has set up some military bases and training camps in Afghanistan, Tajikistan and Pakistan. With the recovery of the Central Asian economy and the forceful striking of all state governments, the influence of religious extremism among the residents has been declining. Under this circumstance, Central Asian religious extremist forces set their base in Afghanistan, and keep disturbing the stability of the political situation by force and terrorist actions, a means adopted by extremist national separatists as well.

By 1999, extremist, terrorist and separatist forces had grown to be a serious practical threat to the whole of Central Asia, mainly as a result of the changing Afghani situation. With the complicated relations among different nationalities, strong religious tradition, an underdeveloped economy, the poor living standard of the local residents, and ill management of the government in some areas, extremist forces have subjected Central Asia to their constant threat. With the support of external forces, extremists caused much disturbance in Tajikistan, Uzbekistan, Kyrgyzstan and Kazakhstan: they set up bases in Afghanistan and the mountainous areas of north Tajikistan, and launched many actions; in most Central Asian states, especially in Kyrgyzstan and Tajikistan, armed extremists crossed borders, attacked villages and took hostages, arousing wide international concern.

Extremist organizations in Central Asia remain active to this today. Not only do the Hizb ut-Tahrir al-Islami (HT) and IMU continue their actions, but there have also emerged new organizations that are even more radical, similar to those in the Middle East and Chechnya. A series of terrorist attacks were launched in Tashkent and Buhala of Uzbekistan in 2004, and the riot in Anjijon, Uzbekistan, in May 2005 was related to extremist forces as well. What deserves special attention is, after both terrorist attacks in Uzbekistan in 2004, a terrorist group named "Jihad" claimed on its website to be responsible, which suggests that extremist and terrorist organizations have been internationalized and become more difficult to control. Although such major extremist forces as the IMU and HT were split after several defeats and will not be able to regroup in a short term, yet the "three forces" will grow rapidly given a new opportunity.

The Worsening Ecological Environment

In the Salt Sea areas, the ecological environment keeps deteriorating, and the water resources are unevenly distributed. The Salt Sea Crisis is one of the most wretched ecological tragedies in the 21st century, directly affecting nearly 35 million residents. Over the past 30 years, the water reserve in the sea has decreased from 1.064 million cubic meters to less than 400 thousand, and the water level has dropped 20 meters, causing such disasters as abnormal climates, soil degradation, as well as sand and salt storms. Statistically, the many sand storms have brought nearly 100 million tons of salt dust in the Salt Sea to the nearby areas, producing a high saline-alkali effect to 80 percent of all arable land in Turkmenistan and a 30 percent reduction of agricultural products in Uzbekistan. Other ecological problems, such as pollution of radioactive materials, exhaustion of water resources, and air pollution, are becoming more serious. For example, a large uranium production base was established in the Ferghana Basin during the Soviet times, and a large amount of nuclear waste was buried right underground, prone to leaking at any time. Regrettably, the international community has not yet paid enough concern to the disastrous ecological problems in Central Asia. On the Consultation Meeting of Aiding Nations to Kyrgyzstan held in Bishkek on October 8, 2002, Kyrgyz President Akayev warned that if timely precautionary measures were not taken in connection with the nuclear waste in the country, then a serious ecological disaster might well occur in the Ferghana Basin and nearby areas at the intersection of Kyrgyzstan, Tajikistan and Uzbekistan.

The Burden of Population Explosion

In view of the large proportion of young people in the Central Asian population, the growth rate of the population will remain high. The scale of population in most Central Asian states has actually exceeded their economic and environmental load, and has generated such problems as surplus labor, a disorderly flow of the population, and serious unemployment. As predicted by the World Bank, the total population of Kazakhstan and Uzbekistan alone will reach 60 million in 2015, while that of all five of the Central Asian states may approximate 90 million. Another problem is the extremely uneven population distribution. At present, the population density of Uzbekistan and Tajikistan has surpassed the world's average standard, 54.0 and 43.2 people per square kilometer, respectively. The population pressure is further amplified by the poor geological and climatic conditions and lack of water resources. In contrast, Kazakhstan, which has the best natural conditions among all Central Asian states, is witnessing a population shortage from population drainage; its population was merely 14.9 million, with a density of only 5.5 people per square kilometer. Moreover, the problems of immigrants and refugees keep plaguing the Central Asian states, and even affect their domestic relations as well as national relations. For example, diplomatic disputes on immigration exist between Tajikistan and Kyrgyzstan; the active smuggling on the borders of Kazakhstan, Uzbekistan and Kyrgyzstan is also related to illegal immigration.

In addition, the Central Asian states are facing an increasingly serious situation in their economic security. First, their economy depends heavily on Western countries; foreign loans of most states have surpassed safe levels. The net foreign loans of Kyrgyzstan reached $1,655 million in 2002, 110 percent of the total GDP, while those of Tajikistan reached $1,016 million at the end of 2001. Even Kazakhstan, the most developed among all Central Asian states, has a heavy burden of foreign loans, which reached $24B at the beginning of 2004, 75 percent of its GDP. Next, many Central Asian states face serious food and energy security problems. Tajikistan and Kyrgyzstan lack such strategic resources as oil and natural gas, while food production cannot suffice Turkmenistan and Tajikistan. Finally, new conflicts over water resources keep emerging between Tajikistan and Kyrgyzstan in the upstream area and the downstream Uzbekistan and Kazakhstan. As most large rivers in Central Asia run across more than one state, disputes over the distribution of water are extremely difficult to resolve.

It can be seen that challenges to Central Asian security are rooted in various aspects, most of which are new, dormant, and internal. A Tajik scholar categorized all the threats to Central Asian security into seven types: 1) a politically radical tendency caused by economic and social crises; 2) geopolitical confrontation and competition over energy and spheres of influence; 3) religious extremist and terrorist tendencies; 4) conflicts among Central Asian states over territory and resources; 5) the ever increasing drug threat; 6) new perturbation caused by the Iraq Crisis; and 7) the development and internationalization of such organizations as the HT. The complicated security situation in Central Asia is closely related to the change of the peripheral or international security situation, thus the issue can hardly be resolved by the efforts of a single or a few Central Asian states.

Pressure On the Security Situation In Central Asia

The stability of Central Asia has long been subject to various traditional and nontraditional threats. Three security crises have occured in the Central Asian states since their independence, namely, the Tajik civil war in 1992; the invasion of extremist forces in 1999; and the turmoil in Kyrgyzstan and Uzbekistan in 2005. All three were regional issues, and none caused large-scale chaos or conflicts, but they clearly indicated the severe security situation of Central Asia. In view of the comprehensive, urgent, and complicated characteristics of Central Asian security, the Central Asian states call for a multilateral cooperation mechanism to safeguard the security and stability of the region.

The Tajik civil war was more or less a result of the political disorder during the later Soviet years, as well as the change of the political situation in Russia, which also caused an agonizing top-level political struggle in other Central Asian states. A direct result of such struggle is the political weakness of the newly independent states. Most Central Asian states had managed to walk out of the quagmire by 1995, with the strengthening of presidential power and the expanding control over the society; compromise among different nationalities in Tajikistan was also partly reached in 1997. Many terrorist attacks plagued Central Asia in 1999. Influenced by the changing Afghani situation and the occupation of the Afghani-Central Asian borders by the Taliban, Afghani extremists invaded the mountainous areas in south Kyrgyzstan, causing much turmoil in the area. In 2000, the IMU based in Afghanistan continued to disturb the regional security situation. After 9/11, the U.S. anti-terrorist actions in Afghanistan have to a certain extent reduced the external pressure on Central Asian security. However, because many extremists and terrorists hid themselves in Central Asia, and such extremist organizations as the HT keep increasing their power, the Central Asian states have fallen into a new security dilemma.

Despite the decreasing external threat to Central Asia since the end of the anti-terrorist war in Afghanistan, Central Asian states are facing even more complicated internal problems, including economic and social instability, conflicts over land and water resources, population explosion, potential clashes between nationalities, border disputes, restrictions on each other's trade and cross-border transportation, religious extremism, corruption, and the ever more serious ecological crisis. All have but proved that Central Asia still confronts various security challenges.

A result of the anti-terrorist war in Afghanistan is U.S.'s military presence in Central Asia and the subsequent intensification of geopolitical competition. The U.S. and its allies signed agreements with Uzbekistan, Tajikistan, Kyrgyzstan and Kazakhstan respectively on the use of some of their airports; they also decided to set a long-term lease on the use of the Hanabad Airport of Uzbekistan and the Manas Airport of Kyrgyzstan. In mid-December 2001, U.S. Assistant Secretary of State Jones said to the Committee on Central Asia and the Caucasus of the U.S. Congress that, the U.S. would not withdraw from Central Asia after the Afghanistan War. In addition, he expounded three major U.S. interests in Central Asia, i.e., preventing the expansion of terrorism, safeguarding political and economic reform and legal institutions in Central Asia, and ensuring the safe and transparent exploitation of Caspian resources. Many Russian and Central Asian scholars believe that the U.S. aims to "kill three birds with one stone," i.e., to exert influence on south Russia, energy-transportation routes, and Xinjiang of China. More specifically, the U.S. aims to use the springboard to control the Caspian region, manipulate the stability of northwest China, curb, or even exclude, Russian and Iranian presence in Central Asia, manipulate the future development of Central Asian states, and set up a pro-American alignment in the region and a pro-American regime in Afghanistan.

Russia held a rather pragmatic attitude toward the U.S.'s entry into Central Asia, a region long considered as Russia's "strategic backyard," and made many unexpected concessions. Russian President Putin said that Russia would not worry about the overall development of U.S.-Central Asia relations, should substantial changes happen to Russia-U.S. security relations. Based on the general objective of Russian diplomacy and the development of the situation, the Russian gesture demonstrates Russia's intention to substantially improve its relations with Western countries with the Central Asian states as its cards to play. Meanwhile, Russia becomes more active in the CIS, striving to maintain its superiority in the region. Both the expansion of U.S. influence in Central Asia and the strategic adjustments of Russia directly affect the security structure of the region. Russia also continues to strengthen its military presence in Central Asia. By setting up a new base in the Kent Military Airport in Kyrgyzstan, Russia aims to pin down the U.S. troops stationed at the Manas Base of Kyrgyzstan. In May 2003, Russia signed an agreement with the Tajik government on establishing a military base in Tajikistan, which was to be expanded on the basis of the original Russian 201 Motorized Brigade; its final goal was to set up a multi-service force, including an airborne branch. In October 2003 and October 2004, Russia formally established a military base in Kyrgyzstan and Tajikistan respectively.

In March 2005, related to the promotion of "democratization" by the U.S. in CIS regions and its encouragement for political dissidents to seize state power, the parliamentary election in Kyrgyzstan gave rise to a political crisis and large-scale turmoil. President Akayev fled, leaving the state out of control. Later in May, Anjijon, Uzbekistan, witnessed prison riots, demonstrations, and even riots in which governmental sectors were overtaken by violence, further indicating the imminence of internal threats that have long been subdued by the "large-power game." The systemic weaknesses, retarded economy and widening social disparities led to the eruption of the accumulated conflicts. As presidential elections are going to be held in other Central Asian states, extremist forces and political dissidents in these states, encouraged by the "3/24

Incident," may cause more instability or even turmoil in Central Asia. The main reasons are as follows:

- Defects in the regimes themselves and the intensification of a power struggle.

The authoritarian regimes in the five Central Asian states inherited some Soviet problems, including the massive bureaucracy and serious corruption, generating more and more social discontent. Moreover, the political structure of the Central Asian states and the parliamentary system are undergoing constant changes, which accrues strong power into the hands of the presidents. However, the long-term control of power by the presidents, as well as of groups with vested interests, may well lead to the suppression of other political parties, thus driving political disputes to the extreme.

- Unsuccessful economic reform and the poor living standard for ordinary people.

The huge gap between the rich and the poor, the unjust distribution of social wealth, and the high rate of unemployment gave rise to sharp social confrontation. In 1998, the number of people living in poverty in the Central Asian states was 28 million, more than half of the total, among whom Uzbekistan and Kazakhstan constituted 30-35 percent, Turkmenistan 50 percent, Kyrgyzstan 60 percent, and Tajikistan over 70 percent. These statistics are very little changed today. Thus, the unbalanced development in the Central Asian economy rendered many areas destitute, especially the mountainous areas, which provides the foundation for the expansion of anti-government actions and religious extremist forces. Kazak President Nazarbayev, worried about the social and economic situation in Central Asia, pointed out that the root of terrorism is poverty, and that globalization is causing more security problems in the region.

- Unsolved nationality and religious issues as "powder barrels."

The Ferghana region is characterized by its complicated relations among nationalities, a backward social economy, and conflicts among nationalities across the borders. Located at the crossing of Uzbekistan, Kyrgyzstan and Tajikistan, the Ferghana has a population of more than 10 million, including half the population of Kyrgyzstan, 20 percent of whom are Uzbeks, 27 percent of the population of Uzbekistan, and 1/3 of the population of Tajikistan (31 percent of whom are Uzbeks)—altogether 8.3 million Uzbeks. The region also has a long Islamic history. Therefore, extremist forces keep causing trouble in the region, in the name of revitalizing the traditional culture and protecting the interests of the minority nationalities.

Geopolitical Factors

With many countries' concerns about Central Asia's unique geographical position and rich resources, as well as various clashes of large-power interests, the geopolitical situation in Central Asia is very complicated, which is a main source of threats to regional security. In this situation, maintaining their position in the large-power competition and avoiding being drawn into international disputes is a big challenge for Central Asian states.

With the change in the regional situation, many other countries besides Russia and the U.S. attempt to expand their influence in the region as well, especially China, the EU, Japan, Turkey and India. Not only do they compete with Russia and the U.S., but they all have their own strategic goals; and they all hope to play a role in the security structure of Central Asia. At present, the security situation of Central Asia is still vague, while domestic problems and non-traditional threats in the Central Asian states are emerging more rapidly. In addition, cooperation led by large states is increasingly active.

Despite the severe security situation in Central Asia, it is still possible to maintain the long-term stability of the region, if the following conditions are met:

- The Central Asian states stabilize and develop their economies gradually. As we know, most of them have serious economic problems and low living standards for most people, apart from the excessive population growth, huge social gaps, corruption, and nationality conflicts.
- The geopolitical situation is ameliorated. Central Asian stability will be destroyed if the situation in Afghanistan again worsens, or new international disputes arise over Caspian issues, or the Chechen War in Russia endures, or acute conflicts erupt between India and Pakistan.
- International cooperation is conducted smoothly in the region. It will be very conducive to regional peace if mutual understanding and cooperation can resolve disputes on the borders over water resources and environments. Otherwise, the

consequences will directly harm regional stability. Moreover, effective international cooperation should also be continued to combat regional extremism and terrorism.

- Large-power relations can be readjusted to a more peaceful paradigm. As Central Asia has its distinctive position in the global and regional strategies of large powers, the power structure and competition over interests will influence the stability of the region from outside.

However, domestic political and economic development in Central Asian states will experience more ups and downs in the future. The authoritarian institution gathers too much power in the hands of the president, which might lead to a successor crisis or a lack of political elites; the burgeoning corruption will harm social stability; nationality and religious problems will continue to plague Central Asian states; and the incumbent regimes will not receive support from the majority of people, due to the large social gaps. Considering that the international environment cannot be improved over a short period, Central Asia's economic prospects are not very promising. Furthermore, there are the problems of increasing foreign debt burdens and very dated technologies, etc. Therefore, it can be predicted that over the coming ten years, the domestic situation in the five Central Asian states can hardly be substantially improved, and may even grow worse. Should that be the case, regional stability would be the first to suffer.

There are but three prospects for Central Asian security, namely, enduring stability; mixed stability and disturbance; and lasting conflicts. The prerequisites for the first prospect are the maintenance of stability in the political situation of the five Central Asian states, effective control of the Afghani situation and international terrorism, as well as the absence of new armed clashes in surrounding areas. The second prospect is actually the continuation of the status quo, in which most Central Asian states will remain stable, with occasional disturbances to a certain state or region from the unstable periphery or extremist forces. In the third prospect, acute conflicts will break out again in Afghanistan and involve Central Asian states, or will lead to constant regime changes and protracted warfare, with the intensification of domestic nationality opposition and political struggle. Even worse, various political and economic crises may arise because of the engagement of external forces and the seizure of state power by religious and national extremist forces.

In the short run, the Central Asian states will not witness a conspicuously improved international environment, but a somewhat worse one, due to many factors: economic conditions in these states cannot be improved completely; a final peace in Afghanistan is still a far-away dream; international terrorism and religious extremism may well thrive again in Central Asia; opposition among different nationalities, as well as national relations in the region, are still very complicated; in addition, the five states still lack the ability to resist external forces. Therefore, the possibility of maintaining the status quo is the most conceivable over the coming five years.

In the mid- and long run, or over the next five years, Central Asia's security situation will improve, mainly for the following reasons: with the increasing power of China and Russia, the Central Asian economy will be promoted as well, apart from the amelioration of the external environment; moreover, out of their own interests, both China and Russia will expect to maintain stability in Central Asia; the institutionalized SCO will play a larger role, while Central Asian states will more effectively combat trans-border crime, with the help of the U.S., Russia, China and Europe; the long-term strategic relations between China, Russia and the U.S. will also help resolve various conflicts in the region by peaceful means, and the five Central Asian states will undertake more global or regional responsibilities accordingly.

There exists also a possibility that the chaos seen in the Middle East in the 20th century will appear in Central Asia, as both share many unfavorable conditions, including complex national and religious issues, the very slow development of social economy, overdependence on the exportation of resources, the competition of large powers in the regions, and the difficulty of controlling the geopolitical situation, and so on. Extremism has continued to threaten Central Asia since the end of the 20th century. Given their proximity to the Middle East and Afghanistan, the Central Asian states can hardly stay away from this threat. Central Asia's future security will still be dominated by large powers, especially the global powers and important nation blocs. As regional actors, the five states will have a long way to go before they can form a united national bloc, thus they will remain passive and subordinate in international and regional affairs for the foreseeable future. It can be predicted that for the next ten years, the counter and balance of various forces in Central Asia will endure, with the common influence of internal and, more importantly, external forces.

Central Asian Influence on China's Security

Central Asia has long been of great significance to the stability of northwest China. During the Han and Tang Dynasties, as Chang'an (Xi'an) was the political and economic center of China, a defense zone was founded in northwest China to protect the city. Defense of the area was even more focused in the Qing Dynasty, as the emperors believed that "its defense is the foundation of stability," and that "if the defense of the northwest can be integrated into the general defense system, China will not worry about any foreign invasion." Therefore, Central Asian security is crucial to the security of Chinese borders and the strategy of the Great West Development.

Historically, all the prosperous periods of China fall in the times when China's surrounding regions, Central Asia included, remained relatively stable. As China's close neighbor, Central Asia shares a long history of communication with China. The stability of the region played a critical role in the foundation of the "Silk Road" and the prosperity of northwest China. During the West Han period, a Chinese delegate named Zhang Qian visited the region and saw a strong Iranian kingdom in Central Asia, which, "as the biggest kingdom in the region, possesses hundreds of cities, and covers hundreds of miles, with very convenient transportation to other kingdoms by the Amu River." Chinese silk was first exported to the Roman Empire through this kingdom, and Buddhism in the region was brought to China during the East Han Dynasty. During the 1st century B.C., the Kuishuang Kingdom was founded, which governed the south of Central Asia. To ensure the safety of the Silk Road and the stability of northwest China, both Han Dynasties set up military offices in the region, which deepened the communication between the region and inland China, and promoted the economic development of the region.

The Silk Road opened the gate for the communication of goods and cultures between the east and the west, in which both northwest China and Central Asia played a crucial role. Almost two millennia later, communication via the Silk Road had been determined by peace in Central Asia and the development of northwest China. In the mid-7th century, the Tang Dynasty defeated West Turkistan, and all small states in Central Asia surrendered to China. Tang's capital, Chang'an, thus became the largest and most prosperous international metropolis at the time, while the economy in the area was booming. After the Arabian Empire conquered Central Asia, the Silk Road stayed busy, exchanging goods as well as cultures. Just as Chinese President Jiang Zemin commented, the ancient Silk Road "is not only a road of trade and civilizations, but a road of friendship and cooperation, which closely connects the Chinese people and the Central Asian people."

After the Song Dynasty, the center of Chinese economy and politics had been moving east; northwest China faced severe security threats from foreign invasions and regional instability. Therefore, the Silk Road went to a decline. The Ming emperors placed more emphasis on the east, having little interest in the development of the northwest or in the connections with Central Asia. Due to the relative peace in Central Asia, the Qing Dynasty inherited the strategy of "migration to the less developed frontiers" and "cultivating the lands by stationing troops" of the Han and Tang dynasties, starting to exploit the region on a large scale and exercising effective management there.

The disturbance of Central Asia in the past century also threatens the stability of northwest China. The aggressive ambition of the Tsar after annexing Central Asia seriously harmed the border security and territorial integrity of northwest China. After Russia's violent suppression of the anti-Tsar national rebellion in 1916, tens of thousands of Central Asian refugees poured into Chinese Xinjiang and placed excessive pressure on Xinjiang security. After the Bolshevik revolution in 1917, Central Asia turned out to be a battlefield for the Red Army and the Belarus Army, the latter fleeing to Xinjiang after their military defeat and threatening Xinjiang security seriously.

Since the independence of Central Asian states, they have adopted a friendly policy towards China, which to a certain extent relieved the military pressure long placed on the northwest Chinese frontiers and improved China's external security environment. However, it also brought about various problems, such as the influence of the political and economic conflicts in Central Asian states over Chinese Xinjiang, as well as the threats to the integrity and stability of China. Therefore, China must remain on guard against all these unstable factors in the complicated Central Asian security situation.

First, the unstable factors directly affect the development of bilateral relations between China and the five Central Asian states. Their total trade volume reached nearly $6 billion in 2004; they also signed many agreements for cooperation in such important programs as energy exploitation, raw-materials processing, as well as pipeline and railway construction, and so on. A lack of guaranteed of security in the region will greatly impede the completion of these programs, thus affecting the realization of their mutual benefits and the development of economic cooperation for west China.

Secondly, the unstable factors harm the stability and security of northwest China, especially Xinjiang. With over 3,000-km common borders and many common cross-border nationalities, northwest China and Central Asia have both benefited from their communication. The long-term stability of the region will create a favorable environment for the development of west China, especially Xinjiang, as well as for the restoration of the ancient Silk Road and friendship of all nationalities in the region. In addition, the economic development of west China needs more foreign investment, which can hardly be conceivable without a stable and safe environment.

Furthermore, due to the proximity of west China and Central Asia, almost all factors that affect Central Asian security will more or less affect west China. Joint actions by both sides are necessary to resolve many common security issues, especially in the nontraditional fields, such as combating transnational crime and a reasonable distribution of water. There are dozens of Uigur political organizations in Central Asia that scheme to separate Xinjiang from China in the name of religion, organizing such terrorist attacks as riots, explosions and homicide. Some organizations, such as the East Turkistan Islamic Movement, keep close ties with the religious extremist forces in Afghanistan and have launched many terrorist attacks in the past few years: in June 2002, the Chinese consul to China's embassy in Kyrgyzstan was assassinated; in March 2003, a Chinese international bus from Bishkek to Kash of Xinjiang was raided and burned, with all 21 passengers killed. Thus, how to combat the three forces, including the East Turkistan separatists, has become one of the major issues in the security cooperation between China and Central

Asian states. China has already signed several bilateral agreements with Kazakhstan and Uzbekistan, and has made some progress over the past.

Finally, the future development of the SCO and its role in Central Asia is a function of the unstable factors. As the first China-initiated regional cooperation organization, the SCO has witnessed China's unique role and has proven crucial to the achievement of China's strategic interests. The changed security situation in Central Asia, such as the U.S. military presence, has posed additional challenges to the SCO. Many Central Asian states have adjusted their foreign policy and security strategy, thus depending less on the SCO.

Conclusions

Central Asia is a region with many security challenges and unstable factors, both external and internal. The security structure of the region has transformed since 9/11, leading to a new round of geopolitical competition, though the fundamental security relations between countries in the region have not been totally reshaped. Facing old and new challenges, Central Asia is in a more complicated security situation. It is natural for China, a neighbor to Central Asia and a country holding many economic and security interests, to be engaged in Central Asian issues.

Central Asia faces an even more severe security situation, which will be further complicated by the competition between various powers and the widening gaps of their security policies and interests. Kazak President Nazarbayev predicted that the next ten years will be "the critical decade" for Central Asia, with more pressing issues of terrorism, extremism, drug trafficking, Caspian energy and collective security waiting to be resolved. The possibility that the chaotic situation of the 20th-century Middle East could be transplanted to Central Asia should not be ignored. The future security structure of the region will still be dominated by large powers, especially global powers and important nation blocs. Whether China can play an active role in the structure is still unknown.

The transformation of the Central Asian security structure directly influences the border security and economic development of west China; some factors are favorable while others are detrimental. Favorable factors include the new development of transnational security cooperation, progress in anti-terrorism in the region, deepening security cooperation between China and Central Asian states, and the broad acknowledgement of China's "New Security Outlook." Unfavorable factors include the increasing nontraditional threats to Central Asian security, the widening gap in Central Asian geopolitics, Western infiltration that impairs China's long-term mutual trust with Central Asian states, as well as the chronic separatist forces. As the stability and development of northwest China is closely related to Central Asian security, China should show more concern over the region in the future.

Chapter Four

Strategic Adjustments and Countermeasures against Extremist Forces of Central Asian Countries after 9/11

Dong Xiaoyang, Su Chang

All Central Asian countries made strategic adjustments after 9/11. First, with their traditional strategy of depending on Russia revised to different degrees, they began to open up to more countries, and to some extent allowed for the intervention of great powers; secondly, they either supported or acquiesced in U.S. military presence in Central Asia for the sake of anti-terrorism, with whose assistance they expected to maintain their own security; thirdly, they adopted "strategic balancing diplomacy" between the U.S. and Russia, as well as other great powers; fourthly, they attempted to develop their economy with the help of great powers. For example, Kazakhstan managed to widen its oil export channels with the aid of Western countries. These strategic adjustments, together with the influence of international and regional factors, gave rise to the shrinkage of traditional Russian strategic space in Central Asia.

After the "Color Revolution" in Georgia, Ukraine and Kyrgyzstan, Central Asian countries are confronted with another round of strategic adjustments, which are yet too early to assess or predict.

Many causes led to the strategic adjustments of Central Asian countries after 9/11. This paper focuses on one of the major factors—concern about anti-terrorism.

I. After 9/11, Central Asia has become the major base for operations and development of extremist forces.

Although the Islamic Movement of Uzbekistan (IMU) was seriously struck after 9/11, the reorganized extremist forces have launched as many terrorist attacks as before. Dispersed terrorists keep reminding Central Asian governments of their "existence" with small-scale attacks. Obviously, religious extremist forces in Central Asia are far from being eradicated. Furthermore, due to the many conflicts arising with the development of the economy and society, the social foundation for extremist and terrorist forces still exists and is even likely to expand.

1. The traditional IMU is separated and reorganized to launch new terrorist attacks, mirrored by Islamic Liberation Party (Hizb ut-Tahrir al-Islami, shortened as the HT in this paper)

Many facts since 9/11 suggest that the IMU is still a potential threat to the security of Central Asia. Its members are now scattered in many areas: 1) in Pakistan, where they remain active on the borders of Pakistan and Afghanistan; 2) in the mountain areas of Afghanistan, where they can launch terrorist attacks with anti-U.S. forces[56]; 3) some of them have returned to Central Asian countries to join the HT; and 4) others have returned to Uzbekistan to surrender to the government. At present, IMU is still an active terrorist force on the Pakistan-Afghanistan borders, and their training camps in the Tajik mountains remain largely intact. The IMU is not yet completely erased in Afghanistan, either, and is still threatening the peace of the local areas with the remnant Taliban forces. The top leader of IMU in Pakistan near Afghanistan borders is still Yuldashev; his son-in-law, Hazeiyev, is the second leader, in charge of IMU finance, while Harricov, another Namanghani, is in charge of hatching terrorist actions. They keep contact with international terrorist organizations and some illegal organizations, and launch guerrilla wars together with anti-U.S. forces on the borders and mountain areas of Afghanistan. Through international terrorist and other illegal organizations, Yuldashev has bought such arms as portable antiaircraft cannons, planning to destroy the air-defense system of the U.S. in Afghanistan.

A most dangerous tendency, however, is the increasing interaction between extremist and terrorist forces in Central Asian countries. At the beginning of 2002, the scattered IMU and Taliban forces began to rally again by uniting other extremists and separatists in Central Asia. Since Islamic extremists in Central Asian countries, Tatarstan

[56] Последователи Джумы Намангани ждут сигнала к выступлению, Век, 13.09.2002, с. 5, Николай Артемов, 14 September 2002.

and Trans-Caucasian countries joined the IMU, the new IMU is divided into groups of 25 to 30 people, and sets up training camps in Pakistani mountains. As Kazakh President Nazarbayev said in July 2002, there were still over 80,000 armed Taliban members within the borders of Afghanistan, and international terrorists were far from being eliminated, all of which posed serious threats to Central Asian security. The IMU forces in Uzbekistan and other countries are not to be underestimated. According to Russian sources, there are still 500 to 600 IMU armed members in Afghanistan, 1,500 in the Tajik mountains, and about 3,000 IMU activists hidden in Ferghana of Uzbekistan[57].

2. The Islamic Liberation Party (the HT)—a new kind of terrorism arises as the major characteristic among religious extremist forces in Central Asia

In 1952, Tachi Nabakhani, a member of Muslim Brotherhood, established the HT in Jordan, or Kuduus in the Middle East, whose predecessor was a branch of the Muslim Brotherhood established in Egypt in 1928, with its first members from Jordan, Syria and Lebanon. This organization was deemed as illegal in all Arab countries, and its followers were closely monitored and politically suppressed, due to its radical claims, terrorist tendency, and, especially, its intransigent attitude towards other organizations. Its aim is to join all Muslims in the world together to found a united Caliph nation. At the beginning of its foundation, this ideal was widespread among young people in Palestine. Before long, the party was banned for its radical and terrorist political aims, its members suppressed or even arrested. Later, the party found its haven in rather tolerant European countries. Headquarters located in London, its members mainly act in the Middle East, Europe and the U.S. Some countries have already settled disputes on the nature of the HT. For example, the party is condemned in Russia as a religious extremist organization with a terrorist tendency[58]; in the U.S., it is also considered as a religious extremist organization.[59]

---

[57] "Facing the Forked Road of Geopolitical Strategy," *Independent Military Observer* (Russia), Vol. 14, 2002.

[58] Виталий Пономарев: Дело активиста "Хизб ут-Тахрир" Юсупа Касимахунова, Правозащитный Центр "Мемориал," 27 February 2004.

[59] Можно ли одними репрессиями победить «Хизб-ут-Тахрир»?, IWPR, Галима Бухарбаеа, Артур Самари, 30 April 2002.

The HT advocates that a united Islamic Caliph nation be established with all Muslims from countries of different social institutions. The major objective of the HT is to fight against infidels, overthrow the present constitutions and institutions in different countries, and seize political power. The HT believes that the most important goal for all Muslims in the world is to establish a united Caliph nation, governed by an elected Caliph. It also believes that all kinds of constitutions, congresses, presidential elections, as well as laws that moderate social relations, belong to paganism. Thus, all modern Muslim countries, including Saudi Arabia, Pakistan and Jordan, are disloyal to Islamic doctrines. The organization features its firm structure, clear guidelines and detailed political agenda. Its ultimate goal is to seize national power, for which purpose three steps are designed. The first step is to publicize the doctrines and claims of the HT by distributing files and pamphlets, as well as establishing basic organizations called "Halekas," each made up of five members. After each Haleka is established, its members set out to found more Halekas, thus developing the organization in a geological order. In the second step, the HT prepares its members to participate in political warfare by further advocating its doctrines and informing its members of world affairs. Finally, the party prepares for the seizure of the political power.

The HT keeps claiming in its propaganda materials that it is a political party rooted in Islam. The actions of HT have a clearly political aspect, instead of merely preaching or admonishment.

The HT opposes the establishment of a secular nation constituted by law, with civil freedoms. Instead, it believes that only Allah (True God) has the right to stipulate laws and grant them to human beings.

The HT maintains contact with Hamas, Jihad, Wahabi, the Muslim Brotherhood, the Armed Islamic Group, and Al-Qaeda led by Bin Laden. On October 9, 2001, after 9/11, in order to support the Taliban's international terrorism, the party announced that "the U.S. and the U.K. Declared War on Islamism and Muslim."

The HT insists that countries all speak Arabic, rather than using their mother tongues.

Since the disintegration of U.S.S.R., the Islamic Liberation Party (HT) has spread into Central Asia.

In 1992, the HT entered Ferghana, Anjijon and Tashkent of Uzbekistan; in 1995 -- Kyrgyzstan; in 1998 -- Tajikistan[60]. The first HT branches were founded in Ferghana, Anjijon and Tashkent during 1992 and 1994, spread to many states in Uzbekistan in a very short time, and reached Tajikistan and Kyrgyzstan during 1995 and 1998. It is also present in Kazakhstan.

In the spring of 1991, Yesomu Abu Muhammad, a Jordanian citizen and representative of the Emir (Chairman) of the HT, Abudulakalim Zalum, went to Tashkent to establish a branch. There he met a Saudi-Arabian student named Yesomu, and went with him to the residence of a man named Abudulashed Kachemov in Anjijon, where he met several people hostile to the Uzbek constitution and institutions. After this meeting, A. Kachemov pledged loyalty to the HT and became the leader of the newly founded underground HT. Subsequently, with the support of Arab students in Tashkent, Yesomu Abu Muhammad, Abudulashed Kachemov, Mulhod Uzmotov, and Hafezolo Nohyulov together founded HT branches in Ferghana, Tashkent, Jizzakh, Sulhanhe Province, and the Xirhe Province.

After the arrest of the top HT leaders in Uzbekistan, party leaders decided to establish organizations in the Sulkin Province of Tajikistan. Abuduzhalir Yusupov and Abuduhorik Muloyev from Wenji Village, Gafrov District of Sulkin Province, joined the party after brief religious training in Anjijon, the former in charge of publicizing the party's doctrines. By meeting laid-off young people aged 18 to 25, as well as poor market vendors, they managed to recruit a large number of people into the party, thus setting up many HT primary organizations in some districts of Sugegin Province.

The HT undergoes rather rapid development in Central Asia.

The International Crisis Commission estimates the number of HT members in

[60] Абдунаби Сатторзода, "Проблемы интеграции исламских организаций в Евроазиатское политическое пространство; О совместимости политического ислама и безапасности в пространстве ОБСЕ," Душанбе 2003, с. 247.

Central Asian countries to be between 15 and 20 thousand[61], mainly in Ferghana, southern Kyrgyzstan, southern Kazakhstan, as well as southern and eastern Tajikistan. The rapid growth of the party largely depends upon its well-disciplined primary organizations named Haleka (meaning "chains"), which is made up of five people, each of whom is to recruit their relatives and friends. The lowest-ranking Haleka members know only members of their groups and know nothing about other groups, and liaison between Halekas is conducted only through Haleka leaders, five of whom are organized into a bigger Haleka, with its own leader. The HT exerts its influence over the public through two classes of people: Islamic religious personnel, especially those considered posterity of the Prophets; and religious teachers. According to the investigative bodies of Kyrgyzstan, the HT is good at disseminating its ideas through teachers who have joined the party; their students and some vendors are subject to their conversion.

The party is mainly composed of young dissidents from the underprivileged class, and more and more people are beginning to support the party. The development of the party in Central Asia can be divided into three periods: the completely non-violence period (from independence to 1996), during which time only religious extremist ideas were spread by passing pamphlets and the preaching of imams in Mosques; the co-existing violence and non-violence period (between 1996 and 2001), while the party was separated into three parts—the HT, Herzban-Nuzla, and Aklamia, the latter two both very radical, believing that Islamization should speed up in Uzbekistan due to complicated internal factors and the government's increasing strikes; the third period starts from 2001 as the party gradually resorts to terrorism.

The HT is a war-like, radical and extremist religious organization.

Its ideas originate from Pan-Islamism, and can be summarized into the following points: 1) the ideal of unification; 2) opposition to democracy, believing that "democracy is evil Western goods and a sinful institution"; 3) opposition against secular regimes, with

[61] Даниил Щипков:"Хизб ут-Тахрир" стремится обратить в ислам весь мир," *Независимая газета-Религии*, 21 April 2004, http://news.ferghana.ru.

pamphlets declaring that "all of us were originally Muslims, but secular regimes separated us into Uzbeks, Tajiks and Kyrgyzs"; and 4) calling for just social institutions and equality among all people, which especially appeals to a large number of Central Asian residents living in poverty.[62]

The HT is a religious extremist organization evolving from radicalism to terrorism. "

Books and pamphlets of the HT reveal that the party must undergo three steps to achieve its goal. In the first and second steps, non-violent means are to be adopted for spreading ideas and establishing branches. In the third step, the party's goal is to overthrow secular regimes through violent means. Major books for spreading the party's ideas include *The Islamic Institutions*; *The Evil Democracy*; *Islamic Politics; The Islamic Society; The Islamic Structure; Islamic Perspectives; Road of the HT*; and *The Organizing Power of Islamism*, etc., which are all translated into many languages and widely disseminated.[63]

3. Central Asian extremist organizations and terrorist organizations tend to unite, joining terrorism to political actions, which poses serious threats to the stability of Central Asia

As reported in autumn 2002, the Central Asian Islamic Movement was founded on the basis of the Islamic Movement of Uzbekistan (IMU), made up of IMU members, some members of the Uzbekistan Liberation Party, Islamic extremists in Tajikistan, Chechen militants, and"East Turkistan" separatists in China.[64] In addition, according to the security agencies of Kyrgyzstan, IMU members in Central Asia, fundamentalists in

[62]Мухиббин Кабири: "ПИВТ и 'Хизб ут-Тахрир': совместимость и различия; О совместимости политического ислама и безапасности в пространстве ОБСЕ," Душанбе 2003.С211-223.

[63] Рахматилло Зойиров, «Стратегия поведения по отношению к 'Хизб ут-Тахрир'; О совместимости политического ислама и безапасности в пространстве ОБСЕ," Душанбе 2003.С224-245.

[64] Website of the Institute of Strategic and Regional Studies directly responsible for the President of Uzbekistan, http://www.uzstrateg.inf, Sept. 10, 2002, quoted from O. Luzhaliyev, "Features of the Islamic Movement in Uzbekistan," *Central Asia and Caucasus* (Sweden), Vol. 3, 2004.

Kyrgyzstan and Tajikistan, as well as Xinjiang separatists, founded a new religious extremist organization named the Central Asian Islamic Movement.[65] Its goal, the same as that of IMU, is to found an Islamic nation with a much broader territory than "a nation in Ferghana areas" as designed by previous religious extremist organizations, including the whole of Central Asia and Northwest China.[66] The headquarters of Central Asian Islamic Movement are located in the mountain areas of Badakhshan Province in Northeast Afghanistan, with rather inconvenient transportation. The Movement's leader is still Yuldashev, leader of IMU, and Al-Qaeda continues to support the Movement, as Bin Laden reportedly helped the organization conceive terrorist attacks.[67]

A new terrorist agenda was soon set after the Central Asian Islamic Movement was founded: [spreading to] southern Kyrgyzstan by the end of 2002, and some other Central Asian countries by spring and summer of 2003--so far without success for some reason. The Central Asian Islamic Movement also targets foreigners living in Central Asia to prove that Central Asian countries are unable to protect the safety of foreigners. According to Stratford Research Center in the U.S., the Central Asian Islamic Movement is hatching a new plan for large-scale attacks.[68] Despite the doubts of many specialists that the Central Asian Islamic Movement exists, it is undeniable that extremists in Central Asia have been reorganized and armed, posing new threats to the stability of all countries.

On July 11, 2003, with regard to the view that "there is no soil for international terrorism in Kazakhstan," N. Dutbayev, Chairman of the Kazakhstan National Security Committee, held a press conference in his headquarters at Astana on the recent security situation of Kazakhstan.

As to the issue of terrorist forces, Dutbayev said that in May 2003 Kazakhstan had unearthed the Almaty branch of the international radical organization, the East Turkistan Islamic Party, and found large stocks of ammunition, as well as home-made explosive equipment confiscated from three arrested members. It was ascertained that they kept

---

[65] Бахтияр Ахмедханов: "Исламское движение Центральной Азии заявило о себе," *Время МН*, 9 October 2002.

[66] Bachgar Ahmedhanov, "Central Asian Islamic Movement," *Time* (Russia), 9 October 2002.

[67] Ибрагим Алибеков: "ИДУ расширяется и готовится к нанесению ударов по Западным мишеням," EURASIANET, 31 October 2002.

[68] Ibid.

contact with other members of the party in many other countries, including Afghanistan, Iran, Uzbekistan, and Kyrgyzstan. Islamic activists of Uzbekistan attempted to legalize themselves in Kazakhstan. Members of the organization were almost as well trained as the special arms in Kazakhstan. HT propaganda leaflets uncovered by Kazakhstan indicate that the organization aims to found an Islamic Caliph country in Central Asia, causing Kazakh authorities to took prompt measures against proselytizers in Kalaganda State and Manjistao State who advocated a"Pure Islamism," under whose influence some Kazakh citizens joined the Taliban. Four Kazakh citizens are still in custody in Guantanamo Bay as POWs, where they told interrogators that they entered Afghanistan only to further appreciate the religion, and that they were engaged only in purely economic business while they were in the Taliban army, or more accurately, in the IMU. At present, Kazakhstan's Ministry of Diplomacy is negotiating with the U.S. about the future of these Kazakh citizens.

II. The HT presents the greatest terrorist threat to the stability and development of Central Asia

The party is an ever-increasing extremist force in Central Asia.

The HT was first founded in Palestine in the 1950s, with the goal of recovering the Islamic way of life and establishing a united Islamic nation, and then founding a united Islamic nation worldwide. The party has become increasingly radical, especially since 9/11, when they called for a "holy war" against the West. The party spread very rapidly in Central Asia, setting up branches in many areas, and advocating the overthrow of current regimes and the founding of an Islamic nation in Central Asia. After the disintegration of the U.S.S.R. in 1991, the HT expanded very rapidly in Hamagan, Ferghana and Tashkent of Uzbekistan, established its first base in Sugeda on the Tajik border one year later, and soon developed in a few states in Kyrgyzstan. Currently, there are over 100,000 members in Uzbekistan alone, and more than 4,000 in Kyrgyzstan, not to mention the larger number of supporters. Because it was deemed responsible for the terrorist explosions in

March and July of 2004, the HT resorts more to violence. Many members propose to overthrow Central Asian regimes by more radical means, such as launching a "holy war."[69] The party's activists are mostly young people with little education and no jobs, thus very discontented with the government. They are also active in recruiting soldiers in Russia and the Chechen areas. On October 9, 2001, they declared their support for the Taliban, believing that "the anti-terrorist war under the leadership of the U.S. and UK is a declaration of war against Muslims and Islamism."[70] The second top leader of Al-Qaeda, al-Zarqawi, who was once a member of the HT in Jordan, later brought the ideas of the party to Iraq. Another leader of Al-Qaeda, Muhammad, kept close ties with the party; another person named Muhammad who killed the journalist Pearl was also influenced by the ideas of HT. [71]

Violent incidents involving the HT are increasing.

The HT is attracting more and more attention. Although it claims to reject violence, the party has turned out to be a conspicuous religious extremist organization in Central Asia. On June 9, 2003, while arresting members of the party, the Russian authorities uncovered a large number of explosives, grenades, and detonators;[72] in 2000, terrorists related to the party caused an explosion in a Protestant church for Koreans in Dushanbe of Tajikistan, killing 9 and wounding 30; the terrorists conducted a chain of assassins in 2001, including of a Vice-Minister for Internal Affairs, the Minister of Culture, and another high-ranking government official; in April, they killed several policemen in the east.

Central Asian countries have begun to take measures against the party.

---

[69] «Вечерний Бишкек».

[70] Бахтиёр Бабаджанов: Религиозно оппозиционные группы в Узбекистане; Религиозный Экстремизм в Центральной Азии: проблемы и персрективы; Организация по безопасности и сотрудничеству в Европе, Миссия в Таджикистане; Материалы конференции Душанбе, 25 апреля 2002г., с. 55-56.

[71] "Дорога от Ташкента до Талибан: группа исламских террористов пытается дестабилизировать союзника США," *The National Review Online*, Зейно Баран, 6 April 2004.

[72] Hong Liang, "121 Terrorists Arrested in Russia," *Global Times*, June 11, 2003, p. 6.

Leaders of some Central Asian countries have expressed their strong resolve to fight against religious extremist forces.

Kazakh President Nazarbayev maintains that drugs, terrorism and limited water resources are major threats to the stability of Central Asia. Thus, he proposes establishing a CIS anti-terrorism center. On February 9, 2001, at the First Plenary Conference of the Army of Kazakhstan, he noted that the greatest threats to national security include terrorism, extremism, invasions by small bandit gangs, as well as drug-related crimes[73].

In April 2002, Uzbek President Karimov announced that Uzbekistan would take more severe measures against the HT. He said the party could not be legalized in Uzbekistan due to its radical and religious extremist nature, and that the Uzbek government would not change its policy on the party, because it violated Uzbek laws.

On May 31, 2002, at the conference on "striking terrorism and religious extremism,"held by Tajik government, in looking back at the situation with terrorism during the previous three years, President Rakhmonov urged all departments of the country to cooperate in the fight against terrorism. The Central Asian countries have taken various measures to strike religious extremist forces. Prior to the explosion in Tashkent on February 16, 1999, and the Hostage Incident in Batkent, Kyrgyzstan, Central Asian countries had mainly adopted a strategy of containment and small-scale raids.

Since 1999, the Central Asian countries have been endeavoring to fight against domestic extremists.[74] Despite the strong measures recently taken by Kazakhstan, Kyrgyzstan, and Tajikistan to stop actions of extremists of the HT, extremist forces in Central Asia develop very rapidly and are becoming increasingly active. High-tech printing equipment was discovered in northern Tajikistan, the number of captured books and pamphlets alone as large as 31,000; some branches of the party were also set up in southern Kazakhstan.

Many Central Asian countries rely on laws and international laws to fight against terrorism and the HT.

---

[73] Zhao Changqing, "Kazakhstan: A Blessed Year in a Favorable Situation," *2001 Almanac of Russia, Eastern European, and Central Asian Countries*, Contemporary World Press, p. 58.
[74] "Наджот," № 33, 2002г.

In August 2000, the Uzbek Congress passed the draft of *Anti-Terrorism Act*, first stipulating anti-terrorism in its law; on October 21, 1999, the *Act on Anti-Terrorism* was issued in Kyrgyzstan, which clarifies anti-terrorist laws and organizations, as well as their different agendas; in July 2001, the President of Kyrgyzstan ratified the *National Security Law*, according to which Kyrgyzstan will support the joint efforts in global and regional security to strike international terrorism, extremism, and sabotage of transportation in Central Asia as well as other regions of the world;[75] the Tajik government believes that under no circumstance should terrorism be appeased, and in 2003, it passed 12 agreements in total on cooperation with the U.N. in the fight against terrorism.

Among all Central Asian countries, Uzbekistan took the strongest measures against religious extremist forces. After the Tashkent explosion in February 1999, the government closely checked members of IMU and HT nationwide, and tried the terrorists engaged in the 2/16 Incident, sentencing six to death; in 2004, Uzbek police caught Zjizibek Kalimov, who created an explosion in the Obilun Market of Bishkek on December 27, 2002, and later sentenced him to death; in January 2005, the Uzbek authorities conducted investigations on six suspects of the explosion in July 2004.[76]

Uzbekistan is trying to put the HT on the Terrorist Blacklist issued by Washington D.C. after 9/11. According to the Uzbek government, the party is recruiting people for terrorist organizations outside Central Asia. At a regional security conference in December 2002, Yeslomov, a representative of Uzbek Ministry of Diplomacy, claimed that the HT carries out extremist actions in most Central Asian countries and poses a threat to Central Asian security.

The security agencies of Tajikistan support Uzbekistan's claims by providing sound proof of the party's terrorist actions. The Tajik government set up official propaganda branches in areas where the party is active, and exchanges ideas with local residents on the party. On Jan. 4, 2001, the Municipal Court of Khuzhan in central Sugeda of

---

[75] Tchemilayev, "National and Regional Strategies, Actions, and Cross-border Cooperation of Kyrgyzstan in International Anti-terrorism," *Collection of the International Symposium on "International Anti-terrorism Situation and Cooperation,"* China International Strategic Society & Hong Kong He Dong Society of International Relations, May 2004.

[76] "В Ташкенте продолжается судебный процесс над организаторами июльских взрывов," ИА Фергана.Ру, Радио Гранд (Ташкент), 21.01.2005 09:18 http://news.ferghana.ru/detail.php?id=599&mode=snews.

Tajikistan sentenced 14 HT members to 8 and 18 years imprisonment respectively, with a charge of engaging in underground activities and fomenting religious and national hatred, and attempting to change the national polity with violence; during 1999 and 2002, 108 HT members were tried in Tajikistan. In 2001, Tajikistan took stronger measures against terrorists, and arrested over 100 HT members, two of whom were later sentenced to death. In addition, Tajikistan endeavored to eliminate domestic extremist forces while the U.S. and other Western countries were attacking the Taliban and Al-Qaeda. Up to 2003, Tajik law enforcement agencies had captured several hundred HT members and prosecuted more than 100. Since January 2003, the security agencies of Tajikistan have been searching Ferghana, and banning unregistered Islamic schools. Over the past 4 years, Tajikistan has arrested 120 radical HT members; 63 clergies were investigated for administrative violation of law at the end of 2002 alone.

Kyrgyzstan adopts milder policies toward the HT than Uzbekistan and Tajikistan.

Although there are over 4,000 members of the party in Kyrgyzstan, very few were actually tried in court. Natalia Shadelova, Vice Chair of the Kyrgyz Committee on Religious Affairs, said that it is dangerous to put the party on the blacklist and suppress it, for the party would only be pushed further to the extreme and made better able to recruit more Muslims. As disclosed by Kyrgyz newspapers on Jan. 19, 2003, only 20 HT members were arrested in Kyrgyzstan.

Kazakh police caught about 40 HT members during a rally in a large mosque in Almaty.[77]

The party keeps close ties with other extremist forces. Its ties with the Xinjiang Independence Movement are especially notable.

---

[77] В Алма-Ате задержаны сторонники исламской организации "Хизб-ут-Тахрир," ИА Фергана.Ру, Радио Свобода, 21 January 2005, 08:39 http://news.ferghana.ru/detail.php?id=596&mode=snews.

According to the security agencies of Uzbekistan, many HT members in Central Asian countries are also members of more notorious international extremist organizations. Shalipov, Vice-Minister of the Tajik National Security Ministry, has stated that there is sufficient evidence to suggest cooperation between the HT and the infamous Aum Supreme Truth.

The HT is not only engaged in terrorist actions, but also in political agitation and riots.

As reported by Russian media, the party played a role both in the Tulip Revolution in Kyrgyzstan in March 2005 and the riot in Anjijon, Uzbekistan. The party in Uzbekistan is also suspected of engaging in drug dealing in Afghanistan. After 9/11, Afghanistan turned out to strengthen its position in drug dealing. The amount of narcotics smuggled from Afghanistan has increased 40 times since the end of the Afghanistan War.[78] Ferghana will become a dangerous spot for terrorism and extremism, as well as a passage route for drug smuggling.

According to some Western analysts, however, the Uzbek government is trying to legalize its cruel suppression of the HT and disguise its large-scale violations of human rights domestically, under the guise of combating international anti-terrorism. Representatives of the Human Rights Society of Uzbekistan assert that the Uzbek government has been persecuting people suspected as members of the party over the past four years, and that even relatives of those people sometimes suffer from severe repression. They worry that Uzbekistan will persecute all banned religious groups and political dissidents even more severely, once the party is put on the blacklist. Professor Cornell of Washington University opposes blacklisting the party, for he thinks it will bring more credit to the party, and thus attract more young people to join it.

As reported by Russia's *Independence* on Nov. 11, 2000, no Western countries have banned the HT, which is declared illegal in Arab and Central Asian countries. The party holds activities openly in the Tokinhash District of London. The leader of the party in UK is a Syrian named Umar Bahari Muhammad, who was arrested by Saudi authorities in

[78] Website of *Truth* (Russia), www.pravda.info, 24 March 2005.

1996 for publicizing religious extremist thoughts and later fled to UK. One of his goals is to establish an Islamic government in the UK.

As reported by *Panorama* of Kazakhstan on July 11, 2003, the International Crisis Commission does not think the HT is engaged in terrorist actions; it contends that the suppression of the party in Uzbekistan is to "find excuses for its refusing political and economic reform," thus likely to render the party more radical. Western specialists believe that for Western interests, influence has to be exerted on the Central Asian countries, especially Uzbekistan, to force them to improve the atmosphere for the existence of the HT.

III. The result of strategic adjustments in Central Asian countries is stronger anti-terror cooperation.

Central Asian countries take constant measures against religious extremism and terrorism mainly to maintain political and social stability, which not only lays a solid foundation for the cooperation of these countries in this field, but also makes it possible for cooperation between them and other countries and organizations. During the first phase, Central Asian countries such as Tajikistan and Kyrgyzstan mainly depended on Russia. Later, some countries turned to China for help, as was shown in the Japanese Hostage Incident in Kyrgyzstan. Since 9/11, Central Asian countries began to cooperate with the U.S. while also strengthening cooperation with other countries. Efforts of Central Asian countries against terrorism have become national, and the traditional strategy of depending on one country has become one of seeking help from many countries.

Cooperation with the United States

The U.S. has been a most important security partner for Central Asian countries, who regard the powerful U.S. military force as the key both to the security of Central Asia and to the balance of influence from such countries as Russia. The U.S. holds clear attitudes toward Central Asian religious extremist forces. The U.S. firmly condemned the terrorist attacks on Uzbekistan and southern Kyrgyzstan in August 2000; later, it named Central Asia as an "anti-terrorist security zone," pledging to undertake responsibility for its security; in December 2000, the U.S. blacklisted the IMU, banning all kinds of aid from American citizens to the organization, prohibiting its members from entering the U.S., and freezing its funds in the U.S. Since their independence, Central Asian countries have benefited from the fast-growing military and security cooperation with the U.S. Their cooperation on combating religious extremist forces is mainly seen in the following aspects:

1. High-level military officials visited each other frequently and signed a number of agreements on military cooperation.

The agreements include yearly cooperation plans, cooperation on military techniques, memos of acknowledgement and cooperation between military departments, plans on helping transform military industries into civil industries, helping Central Asian countries train military officers, and providing military aid and funds, etc. On April 29, 2002, Nazarbayev, President of Kazakhstan, met with the visiting U.S. Secretary of Defense Rumsfeld, and discussed anti-terrorism, among other issues; in August 2002, Gen. Tommy Franks, Commander-in-Chief of U.S. troops in the Middle East and Central Asia, visited Kazakhstan; on Oct. 12, 2001, Uzbekistan and the U.S. jointly announced that the two countries will establish new relations "in order to maintain the long-term security and stability of the region." The announcement states that both governments deem international terrorism a serious threat to global and regional stability. Therefore, they signed an agreement on cooperating to combat terrorism on October 7. On March 11, 2002, Uzbek President Karimov visited the U.S. and, with G.W. Bush, signed the *Uzbekistan-U.S. Agreement on Strategic Partnership and Cooperation*, which ensures joint efforts by both countries to combat all kinds of transnational criminal organizations that threaten national security. In the same year, the Chairman of U.S. Joint Chiefs of Staff, the Vice-Chair of the Joint U.S. Armed Forces Committee, and Commander-in-Chief of the U.S. Central Command, Gen. Franks, all visited Uzbekistan.

2. The U.S. provides aid to the military development of Central Asian countries.

Since 2002, the American Academy of Military Science has begun to train Uzbek military officers, and the Ministries of Defense of both countries have begun cooperation. The U.S. cancelled limitations on military sales to Central Asian countries and exported to them a large quantity of arms, mostly at favorable prices and by means of loans.

3. The U.S. provides military aid to Central Asian countries.

The U.S. has provided much military aid to Central Asian countries to combat religious extremist forces. In April 2000, U.S. Secretary of State Albright visited Kazakhstan, Kyrgyzstan and Uzbekistan, and offered them from 3 million to 10 million USD respectively. In 2002, the U.S. provided military equipment worth tens of millions USD to Kazakhstan. That same year, the U.S. helped Uzbekistan work out a plan on "export inspection and border security," and provided aid of 18 million USD, 14 million of which is used to experiment on an "air sanction" project aiming to strike terrorism and maintain border security. From 2002 to 2003, the U.S. provided Uzbekistan with aid totaling 420 million, 25 million of which is used to improve the combat capability of Uzbek troops.[79]

4. The U.S. and other countries held a joint military exercise.

In August 2002, U.S. and Kazakh troops held a joint military exercise coded as "Balance-Snow Leopard" in Almaty.

5. Central Asian countries support U.S. efforts to strike the Taliban in Afghanistan.

[79]Роман Стрешнев, "США, Европа и Россия--Стратегии в Центральной Азии," *Красная звезда*, 17 August 2004, http://news.ferghana.ru/detail.php?id=3565132771133.3,103,4115536 .

First, leaders of Central Asian countries announced their intentions to "support U.S. actions against terrorists." Secondly, some Central Asian countries allowed land routes for U.S. troops to conduct operations in Afghanistan. For example, Kazakhstan offered to open its air to the U.S.; Uzbekistan opened to U.S. troops its airports, air passages and military facilities; Tajikistan opened its military bases and air, as well as providing field hospitals; Turkey offered land and air passages for the U.S. to transport rescue resources to the Afghan people. Furthermore, some Central Asian countries provided military bases for the U.S. In October 2001, Uzbekistan opened three air bases to the U.S., namely Hanabad, Keked, and Kahgan. At the beginning of November, Tajikistan and the U.S. drew up an agreement by which U.S. troops could use the Khujand, Kulyab and Kurgan-Tyube air bases near the Afghan borders. In December, Kyrgyzstan and the U.S. signed an agreement that the former should provide Manas International Airport for the U.S. as a military base.

Cooperation with Russia

Since 9/11, because Central Asian countries still consider Russia an important key to their security, they have enhanced their cooperation on combating religious extremist forces, which is based on their mutual needs: first, Central Asian religious extremists have strong ties with Chechen bandits, posing threats to the security of both Central Asia and Russia; second, Russia is Central Asia's next-door neighbor; traditional relations between them naturally makes Russia a strong security partner of Central Asia. Uzbek President Karimov said that Russia holds long-term strategic interests in this region, and that it is playing an important role in the geopolitics of Central Asia.[80]

Security cooperation between Central Asian countries and Russia mainly includes:

1. They maintain the same standpoint on combating religious extremist forces and supporting each other.

[80] "Сотрудничество и региональная интеграция отвечают интересам наших народов," *Народное слово*, 2004.6.5.

On August 20, 2000, the presidents of Kazakhstan, Kyrgyzstan, Tajikistan and Uzbekistan met with Ivanov, Secretary of the Russian Federal Security Council, and issued a joint declaration on taking firm measures to fight terrorism. They believe that terrorism and extremism represent a blatant invasion of Central Asia and a shameless violation of the constitutions and democratic principles of the Central Asian countries. On Nov. 29, 2001, Russian President Putin held informal talks with Tajik President Rakhmonov to discuss the cooperation between the two countries on anti-terrorism.

2. Signing contracts on security cooperation.

In December 2002, Russian President Putin and Defense Minister Ivanov made consecutive visits to Kyrgyzstan and signed the *Bishkek Declaration* and *Russia-Kyrgyzstan Agreement on Security Cooperation*, etc. On June 16, 2004, Putin visited Uzbekistan and both leaders signed the *Russia-Uzbekistan Agreement on Strategic Partnership* on the joint actions of both countries to establish an effective security system in Central Asia, granting to each other Most Favorable Nation treatment in trade, Russia's providing Uzbekistan with military supplies, as well as Russia's privilege to use Uzbek military facilities when necessary, and so on.

3. Holding meetings to discuss security measures.

At the informal Russia-Central Asia Summit held in July 2002, leaders of Kazakhstan, Kyrgyzstan, Uzbekistan and Tajikistan met with Putin, and consulted with him about the security situation of Central Asia and international anti-terrorism.

4. Augmenting military bases in Central Asia and maintaining national security together with Central Asian countries.

In December 2002, Russia built an air base at the Kent Airport near Bishkek of Kyrgyzstan. In addition, Russian border troops participate in the defense of the border areas of Tajikistan, in order to combat religious extremists on the Tajikistan-Afghanistan borders and maintain the security of Tajikistan's borders.

5. The Security agencies of both countries cooperate in tracking down religious extremists.

Russia and Uzbekistan cooperate efficiently in fighting against the HT. On Feb. 14, 2003, the Supreme Court of Russia declared the party to be a terrorist organization.[81] On Feb. 13, 2004, security agents of both countries captured one of the leaders of the party, Yusubo Kasimahonov, in Moscow.[82] According to the security department in Russia, the HT exploits many "terrorist tools" of the IMU and maintains contact with Al-Qaeda by sending some members for training in the training camps of Al-Qaeda.

Generally speaking, cooperation between Russia and the Central Asian countries is yet to develop on combating religious extremist forces. After religious extremists attacked Central Asian countries massively in 1999, Russia began to strengthen its cooperation with Central Asian countries in striking religious extremist forces. Despite the close cooperation between the U.S. and Central Asian countries during the U.S.' Afghanistan operation, these countries have realized that Russia is still a trustworthy backup in maintaining regional security. On the other hand, through closer cooperation with Central Asian countries, Russia has consolidated its influence in Central Asia.

Cooperation with China

China and the five Central Asian countries have reached a consensus on maintaining regional security and combating religious extremist forces. As to the terrorist attack in Central Asia in August 2000, China immediately announced its condemnation and its support for Central Asian countries. Both China and these countries are willing to further their military cooperation and take joint measures against religious extremist forces.

---

[81]"Дело активиста "Хизб ут-Тахрир" Юсупа Касимахунова," Правозащитный Центр "Мемориал," Витали Пономарев, 27 February 2004.

[82]"В Москве арестован один из лидеров организации 'Хизб ут-Тахрир'," *Время новостей*, Интерфакс, 17.02.2004.

There are more than ten East Turkistan Independence organizations of different sizes in Central Asia, some of which were founded by Islamic extremists, such as the East Turkistan Islamic Movement that has been declared a terrorist organization by the U.N. In recent years, Xinjiang separatists keep contact with Central Asian religious extremist forces and frequently created incidents targeting Chinese citizens, seriously threatening the security of Northwest China. Therefore, striking religious extremist forces is a mutual requirement for both sides. China and Central Asian countries mainly cooperate in the following aspects:

1. Signing agreements on joint actions to combat terrorism

From December 22 to 25, 2002, Kazakhstan President Nazarbayev visited China and signed with Chinese leaders the *Agreement on Cooperation in Striking Terrorism, Separatism and Extremism*, and the *Agreement on Preventing Dangerous Military Actions*.

2. Holding joint military exercises

On October 10 and 11, 2002, China and Kyrgyzstan held a military exercise on their borders.

3. China provides anti-terrorism aid for Central Asian countries

After the terrorist attacks in Central Asia in 2000, China provided 3-million-RMB in military aid for Uzbekistan, and in October 2003, China provided the security department of Kyrgyzstan with 1 million USD and a significant quantity of computer equipment.

4. Central Asian countries aid China in striking East Turkistan Independence members

In August 2003, the Judiciary Minister of Kyrgyzstan, Osmanov, stated that Kyrgyzstan keeps close watch on East Turkistan Separatism for its ties with the IMU and attempts to destroy the stability of the country. In December 2003, Kulman, First Vice Premier of Kyrgyzstan visited China and held discussions with Chinese leaders on combating East Turkistan Separatism. On Jan. 21, 2004, the Kyrgyz government announced that it would deport several East Turkistan separatists recently caught in Kyrgyzstan to Xinjiang China. In November of the same year, the Supreme Court of Kyrgyzstan declared the Free East Turkistan Organization, the East Turkistan Islamic Movement, and the East Turkistan Islamic Party to be illegal organizations.[83]

Cooperation between Central Asian countries

Central Asian countries maintain that they should work together to counter threats from religious extremist forces in order to preserve the stability of the region. In April 1999, leaders of the five Central Asian countries insisted in a joint declaration that they would adopt measures to maintain regional peace and security. On April 21, 2000, Kazakhstan, Uzbekistan, Kyrgyzstan and Tajikistan signed an accord on striking religious extremism, terrorism, transnational organized crime, and other actions that threaten regional stability and security; in August 2000, the presidents of the four countries made a joint declaration on seeking closer ties against international terrorism; in the same month, leaders of the law-enforcement departments of Uzbekistan, Kyrgyzstan and Tajikistan met in Kyrgyzstan to formulate specific measures to strike international terrorists; on Jan. 5, 2001, four national leaders of the Central Asia Economic Community held a conference in Almaty and proposed measures to prevent international terrorists from causing further damage in Central Asia.

After 9/11, the Central Asian countries continued their cooperation on striking religious extremist forces, believing that remnant IMU members still threaten Central Asian security. They also began to focus on striking the HT. Tajikistan proposed that all

[83]"Преследования уйгуров на территории Киргизии лежит на совести Китая," Eurasianet, Бакыт Ибраимов, 30 January 2004, http://www.eurasianet.org.

Central Asian governments sign an agreement on jointly striking the party.[84] Central Asian cooperation primarily involves the following means:

1. Holding conferences on regional security

On Feb. 28, 2002, leaders from Kazakhstan, Uzbekistan, Kyrgyzstan and Tajikistan attended a conference of the Central Asian Cooperation Organization in Almaty to discuss further cooperation on security and stability. On June 4, the first Leadership Conference of "Yatsin Conference" was held in Almaty, at which the presidents of Kazakhstan, Uzbekistan, Kyrgyzstan and Tajikistan, as well as leaders of other nations, published the *Almaty Papers* and the *Declaration on Eliminating Terrorism and Promoting Dialogue between Civilizations*, both aimed at enhancing Asian peace, security and stability. From June 6 to 7, an informal summit of member nations in the Central Asian Cooperation Organization was held in Aktau, Kazakhstan, mainly concerning Central Asian security and stability.

2. Improving the regional security cooperation system

On Feb. 28, 2002, Kazakhstan, Uzbekistan, Kyrgyzstan and Tajikistan founded the Central Asian Cooperation Organization, whose predecessor was Central Asian Economic Community. The new organization focuses on cooperation on security and regional issues. On Dec. 27, 2002, leaders of the four member-nations held a conference in Astana, Kazakhstan, and declared that they will endeavor to cooperate comprehensively to fight drug trafficking and cut off this major financial resource for international terrorist organizations.

Cooperation under the Shanghai Cooperation Organization (SCO)

---

[84] Рахматилло Зойиров, "Стратегия поведения по отношению к 'Хизб ут-Тахрир', О совместимости политического ислама и безапасности в пространстве ОБСЕ," Душанбе 2003, s. 224-245.

Since the founding of the SCO, cooperation of all member-countries has grown rapidly on striking religious extremism, as manifested in the following ways:

1. The member-countries signed many legal documents on anti-terrorist cooperation and established a new outlook on security, laying the legal basis for joint anti-terrorist actions.

A new security outlook based on mutual trust, mutual benefit, equality and cooperation forms the basis for the SCO. After 9/11, the SCO began to strengthen cooperation on security issues and signed a series of legal documents to improve mutual trust in the military arena and enhance cooperation. On June 15, 2001, leaders of China, Russia, Kazakhstan, Uzbekistan, Kyrgyzstan and Tajikistan signed *The Shanghai Pact on Striking Terrorism, Separatism, and Extremism*, which has proven a key step in furthering cooperation among these countries, and provides a legal basis for maintaining regional security and stability, as well as combating the "three forces" [of terrorism, extremism and separatism]. On June 7, 2002, they also signed the *Charter of the SCO* and the *Agreement on Regional Anti-Terrorist Organizations*, expressing their resolve to fight against all forms of terrorism, separatism and extremism.

2. Improving the multilateral anti-terrorist cooperation system. Departments of National Security and Defense of all member states meet periodically to discuss measures against terrorism.

In May 2002, leaders of security agencies in the SCO countries held a routine meeting in Astana, proposing starting a regional anti-terrorist institution as soon as possible and broadening their cooperation with specific measures. In the same month, defense ministers of SCO countries met in Moscow and exchanged views on further developing military cooperation.

The multilateral anti-terrorism cooperation system is also improving.

In January 2004, the SCO Secretariat was established in Beijing; the SCO Regional Anti-terrorist Implementation Committee was founded in Tashkent in June, which means that the multilateral organization has begun to function in its true sense.

3. Holding military exercises to accumulate experience for joint anti-terrorist actions.

The SCO has successfully held bilateral and multilateral joint military exercises for more vitality and practice. In October 2002, China and Kyrgyzstan held an anti-terrorist exercise coded "01" on their borders; in August 2003, troops from SCO members held an exercise coded "United-2003" in Kazakhstan and China, which indicates the resolve of SCO countries in fighting religious extremism.

Cooperation within the framework of Commonwealth of Independent States (CIS)

1. CIS Collective Security Treaty Organization

In order to maintain regional stability, most Central Asian countries bolster the security cooperation system led by Russia and play an active part in the CIS Collective Security Treaty Organization, which is considered crucial in ensuring the security of the southern CIS borders.[85]

During the U.S. air attack on Afghanistan on Oct. 8 and 9, 2001, as suggested by Tajikistan, the secretaries of the security conference of members of CIS Collective Security Treaty Organization held a meeting on anti-terrorism in Tajikistan's capital, Dushanbe, and passed a joint declaration on the common standpoint of the countries on counter-terrorism, as well as specifying their counter-terrorist measures. It was stated in the declaration that the social foundation of international terrorism must be uprooted, the economic foundation being the first. Participants of the meeting decided to enhance

[85] China News Agency reports from Almaty, Sept. 17, <http://online.cri.com.cn/772/2002-9-18/68@93269.htm>.

cooperation between the intelligence agencies of these countries in the exchange of intelligence about terrorist bases and their active areas.[86]

On Nov. 28, 2001, a Conference of Foreign Ministers for member-countries of the CIS Collective Security Treaty Organization was held in Moscow, at which it was proposed that a widely represented government be established in Afghanistan to eradicate terrorist bases and eliminate organized and drug-related crime. In April 2002, the CIS Counter-terrorist Center conducted a military exercise in Kyrgyzstan and Tajikistan coded "South-Anti-terrorism-2002" joined by troops from Russia, Kyrgyzstan, Tajikistan and Kazakhstan, in order to strengthen their cooperation and reaction capacities to international terrorist attacks.

On May 14, 2002, the Council of CIS Collective Security Treaty Organization passed a resolution in Moscow that changed CIS Collective Security Treaty to the CIS Collective Security Treaty Organization. The presidents of Kazakhstan, Kyrgyzstan and Tajikistan, as well as leaders of other countries, attended the conference and decided to further military cooperation among members of the organization by establishing a joint military administrative institution and a collective force for prompt reaction to terrorist attacks. On Nov. 20, the group's member-countries decided to increase their military forces in Central Asia. In December, the Fifth Conference of Security Secretaries of Contract Members was held in Bishkek, mainly discussing the enhancement of military force in Central Asia and the improvement of a joint mobile force. Russian Security Secretary Luzayelo said that Russia has taken a series of joint measures with Central Asian countries to heighten their cooperation in counter-terrorist and anti-drug efforts.

2. Counter-terrorist Military Exercises within the Framework of CIS

Despite the many problems confronted by CIS in its own development and the difficulty in its integration, the CIS still has a key part in maintaining security. On Oct. 7, 2002, a CIS Summit Conference was held in Chisinau, capital of Moldova, at which a memo for a joint counter-terrorism program was signed, specifying cooperation on the

---

[86] "Representatives of CIS Collective Security Treaty members held consultations," *Reports on Foreign Affairs* (Russia), November 2001, Vol. 11.

borders of the member-countries, planning on their joint actions to fight crime between 2003 and 2004, as well as reaching an agreement to enhance the air-defense system of CIS members. From June to August 2003, Kazakhstan, Kyrgyzstan, Uzbekistan and Tajikistan joined in a CIS joint air-defense exercise coded "Fighting Coordination-2003," the second phase of which was held in Kazakhstan and Uzbekistan. The CIS counter-terrorist center has also held a series of counter-terrorist exercises in Central Asia. In summer 2003 too, Kazakhstan, Russia, and Ukraine held a military exercise named "2003 Calling for Counter-terrorism."

3. Counter-terrorist issues are actively studied within the framework of CIS.

On Nov. 10 and 11, 2003, as proposed by the Kazakhstan National Security Council, an International Symposium on Joint Anti-terrorism was held in Almaty, joined by staff from the CIS Counter-terrorist Center, staff of security agencies from Kazakhstan, Kyrgyzstan, Tajikistan, Uzbekistan, Russia and Ukraine, staff of the State Security Council, Presidential Security Bureau, National Security Council, and Department of Internal Affairs of Kazakhstan, as well as political scientists specializing in anti-terrorist studies.

At the symposium, causes for the development of terrorism were explored, while means of surveillance of international terrorists and extremists, as well as measures to counteract them, were discussed. Attendees also exchanged views on maintaining the security of strategic targets, improving CIS anti-terrorist measures, and enhancing cooperation among the security agencies of CIS members.

The symposium approved cooperation among CIS-member security agencies. With the example of the capture of a terrorist active in Central Asia and Turkey through the joint efforts of Kazakhstan and Kyrgyzstan, as well as the example of the cooperation of Kazakhstan and Russia in detaining Chechen terrorists, Vice-Chairman of Kazakhstan National Security Council Borek emphasized the necessity of their cooperation. He disclosed that Kazakhstan was making a list of terrorist organizations in the country, and that Kazakhstan has increased funding to enhance the protection of key targets and facilities.

Mr. Sachekov, head of the CIS Anti-terrorist Center, noted the many explanations for terrorism, for which a definition committee was established in the center. He pointed out that the task of the center has been to coordinate the counter-terrorist actions of security agencies of all countries, analyze security conditions for CIS and the world, coordinate actions of the U.N. Anti-terrorist Committee, publicize the anti-terrorist experience of other countries in the CIS, as well as to train CIS security agents.

IV. Factors that may cause Central Asia to readjust their strategies.

Central Asian countries are in a transitional period in politics, the economy and society, all of which are seeing rapid changes. The dynamics poses real and potential challenges to the stability and development of Central Asian countries. Hence, it is necessary to adjust policies and strategies accordingly.

After the Color Revolution of Kyrgyzstan, Kyrgyzstan and Uzbekistan sent a strong signal for the readjustment of their strategy by asking the U.S. and NATO to set a timetable for withdrawing their troops.

Many factors may cause Central Asia to readjust its strategies, which can be classified into those concerning extremist and terrorist forces, and those concerning the Color Revolution, both of which are quite active in Central Asia.

Factors concerning extremist and terrorist forces:

After the Color Revolution in Ukraine, Georgia, and especially Kyrgyzstan, Islamic terrorists took the opportunity to seize political power, grow and become active. For example, the HT participated in the Color Revolution in Kyrgyzstan through some radical actions. According to Uzbek and Russian sources, the HT also joined in the riot in Anjijon, Uzbekistan.

The problem now is, if extremism and terrorism cannot be uprooted by the U.S., NATO, CIS Collective Security Treaty members, or the SCO, then opportunities remain for extremism and terrorism to become active again; besides, the Central Asian countries may well lose their patience in international cooperation.

As stated above, the biggest real and potential threat to Central Asian security is the HT. The following conditions may cause the HT's further development:

1. Because the Color Revolution in Central Asian countries has just begun, extremist and terrorist forces can play a role in attacking the present regimes.

2. The U.S. and other Western countries have not yet decided on the nature of the HT, which leaves room for the development of such organizations.

3. Extremism and terrorism are closely connected with drug smuggling. As seen from above, drug production and smuggling increased many times after the Afghanistan War as a financial guarantee for extremists and terrorists, while the U.S. troops in Afghanistan focus on fighting against terrorist organizations, unable to stop drug smuggling in this area efficiently. Therefore, Central Asia has become a major passage route for drug smuggling, and drug dealers garner total yearly profits as high as 2.2 billion U.S. dollars.

4. Through drug smuggling, extremist and terrorist forces may have controlled Osh in southern Kyrgyzstan, and the whole Ferghana and its surrounding areas, and they may even build a second base for drug production and transportation after Afghanistan, moving the Afghanistan base 1,000 km northward. If the need arises, such a base could be used for terrorists and extremists.

5. The regionalizing and internationalizing tendency of the HT makes it a big threat to Central Asian countries and even surrounding areas. The party is transnational and trans-regional, whose aim is to Islamize the whole of Central Asia and found a united Islamic nation. The party is active in other countries of the world too, such as founding its headquarters in London, setting up branching in Xinjiang China and engaging in sabotage, as well as acting in Laganda and Manjistao of Kazakhstan. Therefore, such extremist and terrorist organizations as the HT should not be studied only on the context of one country.

Factors concerning the Color Revolution:

Because the U.S. and some other countries are not satisfied with the democratization process of Central Asian countries, they encourage these countries toward political transformation by supporting or acquiescing in rather radical means of change and the Color Revolution.

Conflicts arising during the transformation of Central Asian countries are the social foundation for the Western encouragement of the Color Revolution. Such conflicts include the huge proportion of poor people in the society (constituting 30 percent or even higher in Tajikistan, Kyrgyzstan and Uzbekistan), serious unemployment, official corruption, nepotism, a crisis of national identity, and the slow improvement of public living standard, etc. Meanwhile, the opposing forces in Central Asian countries continue to seek support from abroad.

Next, let's examine the countries in which the Color Revolution has taken place.

1. Ukraine, Georgia, and Kyrgyzstan have not completed revising their Russian policy, by which they will continue to depend on Russia;

2. The political institutions of the three countries have not yet changed with the Color Revolution to be more democratic;

3. Because these countries may remain unstable during the transition period, the U.S. interests in the region can hardly be fully realized with the shift of regimes, as in the examples of Latin America and Africa. U.S. intervention even caused the separation and instability of Latin America.

4. Unlike that in Ukraine and Georgia, the Color Revolution in Kyrgyzstan happened in a violent way, and resulted in a parliament that had led to the revolution previously, which gave rise to confusion and frustration in the society. Besides, riots may happen any time in Kyrgyzstan because of its social and political instability. The imbalance of interest redistribution after the revolution may also cause new conflicts. Furthermore, the political institution of Kyrgyzstan has far to reach U.S. democratic standards, even after Akayev's departure.

If the Color Revolution proceeds in other Central Asian countries, which is very likely at present, then more elections will be seen in Central Asia, supported by the opposing forces and other forces, and the revolution may well come about through violence or riots. At least from present perspectives, the violent mode is hard to avoid, which poses the following threats and challenges:

1. Central Asian countries have universally become cautious toward the Color Revolution; some countries have even adopted control measures to maintain their [current] political institution and the interests of the authorities. Will that lead to a readjustment in the political transformation strategies of Central Asian countries?

2. Many national and tribal conflicts exist in Central Asian countries, which may cause violent clashes in a violent transformation mode;

3. Central Asian countries are very sensitive to external influence. Will they be forced to turn to Russia for protection if they resist U.S. and Western support of the Color Revolution?

4. The Moldova Mode. Challenged by the Color Revolution, Moldova chose to seek further help from the U.S., without changing its original institution. Yet Central Asian countries are not very likely to adopt this mode, because they can hardly control the process if the Color Revolution happens, and violence will be bound to dominate.

In the context of the Color Revolution, the above-mentioned two factors may interact with each other, or even integrate, the result of which would pose serious challenges to Central Asia, the surrounding nations, as well as to the U.S. and the West.

It has been seen from the Color Revolution in Kyrgyzstan that the previous regime can be overthrown by street democracy and violence, yet what will be the new institution like?

Extremism and terrorism may revive in Central Asia, not only in the society, but also within the regime, i.e., extremist and terrorist regimes may arise in Central Asia.

Consider the situation in Uzbekistan. The Anjijon case can almost be regarded as a preview of the Color Revolution in Uzbekistan. Although there are no mature opposing forces in the country, terrorist organizations and extremist forces exist in Uzbekistan. If the authorities cannot control the situation, then extremist and terrorist forces are very likely to seize the power.

What will be the consequences?

Unlike the radical democratic reform and transformation expected by the U.S. and the West, the result will be the seizure of power by terrorist and extremist forces in Central Asia.

Uzbekistan and Tajikistan will then become the second and the third Afghanistan and Taliban, while Central Asia and Afghanistan will be united, and Afghanistan will be controlled by another Taliban-like regime. If so, Central Asia will become a new base for international terrorism, which threatens not only U.S. and Western interests in Central Asia, but also Russian interests and the security of West China.

Therefore, Central Asia is likely to readjust its strategy. The advance of the Color Revolution may not benefit the U.S. and the West; neither can it immediately generate democratic institutions as expected by the U.S. and the West. On the contrary, it may bring about instability and riots, and even control by extremism and terrorism.

A few conclusions:

Central Asian countries are in a period of social transformation and have their own political and cultural characteristics. The transformation process must abide by the general laws of social transformation; no radical means can guarantee expected results.

Stability and development are most important to Central Asia and are essential to regional security. The major threats to Central Asia remain extremism and terrorism, which should be the top concern of the international community. Extremist and terrorist forces may start turmoil and riots by exploiting street politics and the Color Revolution, which may lead to large-scale Islamic revolution. As we know, revolution in Iran led to an Islamic regime, while that in Afghanistan brought about the Taliban.

In order to eliminate extremism and terrorism, it is necessary to promote stability and development, improve the living standard of the people, and further press for reform by law, giving full consideration to the characteristics of the social institutions of Central Asia.

The stability and development of Central Asia are beneficial to China and other major powers that maintain influence in the region, as well as to the security of Central Asia.

Chapter Five

Recent Development and Prospects of Relations Between China and the Central Asian States

Shi Ze

Surrounding west China, Central Asia has grown to be an important new geopolitical region since 9/11. Despite the rapid changes in the geopolitical situation in the region during the previous years, the relationship between China and the Central Asian states has developed steadily in all fields, which is among the credits of China's diplomacy with surrounding nations.

China's Central Asia Policy

The Central Asian states respond actively to China's foreign policy of "Friendship, Stability and Mutual Prosperity with Neighboring Countries," and their mutual political trust has been further strengthened.

First, summit meetings and communication in various fields have been institutionalized between China and the Central Asian states. Leaders of both sides have visited each other frequently in the past years: President Hu Jintao and Premier Wen Jiabao visited Central Asia and attended the summit meetings of the SCO each year; Kazak President Nazarbayev visited China twice last year [2004]; Uzbek President Karimov visited China not long ago; and each year, Foreign Minister Li Zhaoxing visited Central Asian states and met with foreign ministers of other states at the Conference on Interaction and Confidence Building Measures in Asia (CICA) and the SCO. In general, both sides have kept close contact with each other in such fields as diplomacy, trade, culture and security, coupled with the growing interaction between the congresses, parties, local governments and peoples of China and Central Asian states.

Second, on the basis of reciprocity and mutual understanding, the two sides have successfully resolved their border disputes. Since the settlement of China-Kazakhstan border disputes, China has signed an agreement with Kyrgyzstan on border definition. China also signed *The Supplementary Agreement on Border Definition* with Tajikistan, which was ratified by both countries last year. By now, the 3,300-km borderline between China and the Central Asian states has been completely defined.

Third, China has signed treaties of friendship and cooperation with most Central Asian states, further strengthening the legal foundation for the development of their relations. After the signing of the China-Kazakhstan and China-Kyrgyzstan treaties, President Hu visited Uzbekistan in June 2004, and signed with Uzbek President on *The Joint Declaration on Further Developing and Deepening the Friendly Partnership between Both Countries*, changing their past "friendly relationship" into "friendly partnership," and they signed *The China-Uzbekistan Peaceful and Friendly Cooperation Treaty* when the Uzbek President visited China in May 2005.

Last, both sides have begun to highlight and develop their cooperation in the realm of security. In recent years, China has signed cooperation agreements with Kazakhstan, Kyrgyzstan, Uzbekistan and Tajikistan on striking the "three forces" [of terrorism, separatism and extremism], for better coordination of their actions and for sharing intelligence. Within the framework of the SCO, China and the Central Asian states have held several joint military exercises targeted at terrorist forces and strengthened cooperation on such non-traditional security issues as striking transnational crime and drug dealing. In July 2005, all SCO members signed *The Compendium on Cooperation in Striking the Three Forces* at the Astana Summit Meeting. Moreover, communication and cooperation between China and the Central Asian states also tend to be further enhanced.

Mutual Advantages

The geopolitical advantage of China and Central Asia, as well as the potential for complementary economies, is becoming manifest.

The biggest advantage for both sides in developing relations is their close proximity. After the successful resolution of the border disputes between China and Kazakhstan, Kyrgyzstan, as well as Tajikistan, the 3,300-km borderline has turned out to be a crucial link between them, whose transportation conditions are also rapidly improving. Direct flights to the capitals of all five Central Asian states have been opened, while there are several flights to Kazakhstan, Kyrgyzstan, and Uzbekistan each week; direct flights to Tajikistan and Turkmenistan ended the period of history when transportation had to pass through a third country. Moreover, the China-Kazakhstan railway, as well as the China-Kyrgyzstan and China-Tajikistan roads, undertake an increasing amount of transportation, with road conditions improving. Compared with the 5 million tons of transportation through the Alas Mountain Port between China and Kazakhstan only a few years ago, the current transportation capacity has reached 10 million tons, but it still cannot meet the needs of the sharply increasing amount of goods. While inspecting the port not long ago, Kazak President Nazarbayev suggested raising the transportation capacity to 15 million tons by 2010. With China's aid of 60 million RMB, the construction of the China-Kyrgyzstan-Uzbekistan Road has been started in Kyrgyzstan. Further, China and Kazakhstan have a plan to construct a standardized railway that connects Europe with both countries. Also notable is the opening of the Karasu Port between China and Tajikistan on the Pamir Highland in May 2004, which opened the long-closed window between China and the southern part of Central Asia. Compared with 10 years ago, China and the Central Asian states are witnessing improved conditions and doubling amounts of transportation, as well as an accelerated flow of goods, people and information, which greatly promotes communication and cooperation between both sides. With the improvement of transportation conditions, cooperation between China and the Central Asian states in recent years is on its way to transforming the complementary potential of their economies into practical implementation of their respective advantages.

A Growing Economy

The improvement of Central Asia's economy is providing new opportunities to expand economic and trade cooperation between both sides.

A hindering factor in China-Central Asia economic and trade cooperation had been the enduring economic depression of the Central Asian states since their independence. In the late 1990s, the GDP of most Central Asian states was less than half of that before the disintegration of the Soviet Union. Such a phenomenon has now changed greatly over previous years.

First, the economy of the Central Asian states has continued to recover over the past few years. The global economic recovery and the rising price of energy, and especially the conspicuous improvement of the Russian economy, have provided a much better environment for the economic development of Central Asian states than a few years ago. Meanwhile, the relatively stable domestic political situation and consistent transformation in these states also contributes to their economic growth. The growth rate in most states was over 10 percent in 2003, while that of Turkmenistan even exceeded 20 percent. The total GDP of the five states has reached $58 billion, $27 billion of which was contributed by Kazakhstan alone. These states also are witnessing a rapid growth of financial revenues and gold reserves, which are $5 billion for Kazakhstan and $4 billion for Turkmenistan. Besides, the average income in all the states has also increased (by more than $2,000 in Kazakhstan), resulting in a higher living standard for the populace.

Second, the environment for investment in Central Asia has further improved. At present, the Central Asian economy is at a turning point between recovery and development, thanks to the accelerated process of reform and improvements in the legal system. All the states have formulated a long-term strategy for development: *The New Investment Law* and *The Land Law* in Kazakhstan; *Strategy for Political, Economic and Cultural Development* by 2020 in Turkmenistan; and *Strategy for Economic Development by 2015* in Tajikistan. Furthermore, a large amount of foreign investment is introduced into these states; such international financial institutions as the World Bank, the Bank of Asia and the Bank of the European Union also provide many loans. With the improved economic environment, as well as new opportunities arising from the new strategy for development of Central Asian states, transnational companies are also planning to increase their investment in the region.

Third, the volume of trade between the Central Asian states and other states has been rising. In record-setting 2003, the trade volume of Kazakhstan reached $21 billion, an increase of 30 percent, while that of Turkmenistan also reached $6.1 billion; trade volume of other Central Asian states also increased considerably. With the large amount of foreign investment, many large- and middle-scale joint projects have been started with satisfactory benefits.

The positive changes in the Central Asian economy greatly promote economic cooperation between China and these states. Statistics shows that trade between both sides has increased by more than ten times over the past 12 years, from $0.47 billion in 1992 to $4 billion in 2003, and to $5 billion in 2004, $4.5 billion of which was between China and Kazakhstan. In addition, China's exports to Central Asian states has exceeded its imports after many years of an adverse balance of trade.

Because of the change of the export structure, economic cooperation has been expanded from the field of trade only to the fields of techniques and investment. China's investment in Central Asia has reached $1 billion to date, and many joint programs have been, or will be, completed: the China-Kazakhstan joint construction of the Atasu-Alas Mountain Pass Oil Pipeline started on September 28, 2004, and is to be completed at the end of 2005, while both countries are planning to construct another pipeline for natural gas, which will also promote their energy cooperation; China and Uzbekistan cooperate well on such programs as electric locomotives, tractors and gas meters, and during the visit of the Uzbek President to China this year, both sides signed an agreement on energy cooperation, by which China is to invest $600 million in Uzbekistan in various programs; the joint paper mill of China and Kyrgyzstan has also begun to run, and last September [2004], leaders of both countries signed *The 2003—2004 Compendium on Cooperation,* which lays a good foundation for their further cooperation; China's irrigation techniques and telephone-network upgrading program in Tajikistan produced good results too. In addition, China has exported a lot of petroleum-producing machinery to Turkmenistan over the years, and they have begun to cooperate on restoring oil wells. Trade between China and Central Asia exceeded $5 billion in 2004, only 1/12 of the $5.8 billion total trade volume of Central Asia, thus indicating great potentials for their further cooperation. The continuous development of the Central Asian economy will undoubtedly lay an even more solid foundation for the further development of their trade and friendly relations, especially after the visit of Chinese Vice-Premier Wu Yi to four Central Asian states at the end of last July.

SCO Outreach

The SCO has strongly promoted China's cooperation with Russia and the Central Asian states.

As a new multilateral cooperation mechanism designed to overcome the limitation of bilateral cooperation, the SCO was created by China and other member states through many years' exploration under rapidly changing world conditions. Since its founding, it has greatly promoted the general relationship between China and the Central Asian states. All its member states favor the "Shanghai Spirit" of mutual trust and mutual benefit, cooperation on an equal footing, respect for diverse cultures, common development, the new security outlook and new modes of international relations and regional cooperation. Having accomplished its initial foundation tasks, and focusing on economic and security cooperation, the SCO has begun its overall development and substantial cooperation in combating the "three forces" and on economy and trade, thus contributing very much to the peace, stability and prosperity of the region. At the Bishkek Summit Meeting last September, all member states passed the *Plans on Measures to Implement the Compendium of Cooperation on Economy and Trade*, which concerns their cooperation in 127 programs in 11 fields, including transportation, energy, telecommunications and agriculture. The viable cooperation mechanism and forward-looking designing of the SCO has already demonstrated its significance. Reality shows that the SCO accords with the interests of all member states, who, by effective cooperation, have also strengthened their friendly relationship.

Prospects of Relations Between China and the Central Asian States

Since the establishment of formal relations between China and the Central Asian states, their relationship has been developing steadily, mainly because of their broad consensus and common interests.

In terms of politics, at first, both sides put their emphasis on economic construction and creating a favorable international environment for their domestic economies; next, each regards the other as a friend, and each pursues the policy of equality, mutual respect for each other's choice, non-interference in each other's domestic affairs, friendly consultation, mutual trust and tolerance, by which they have managed to solve long-standing border disputes; thirdly, both China and the Central Asian states advocate establishing a just and democratic multilateral order based on well-acknowledged international laws; they both strive to promote the democratization of international relations and the diversification of modes for development, as well as the stable and harmonious development of Central Asia.

In the economic field, each side has market demands on the other, and the sides complement each other, with great potential for their further development: China's "West Development and Outreach ['Going-Out'] Strategy" is quite compatible with the Central Asian states' economic development strategy. China is more advanced in light industry, machinery, techniques and agriculture, while the Central Asian states are rich in energy and other resources, as well as in husbandry. As inland states, Central Asian states need to enter the Asia-Pacific market with China's help, while promoting their economies using China's techniques and capital. Similarly, with the rapid economic development, China needs to import more energy and other resources from Central Asia, as well as to have a greater share in the Central Asian market. With the completion of China-Central Asia transportation and the construction of more ports in subsequent years, a transportation network that connects China and Central Asia from north to south is to be established through the joint efforts of both sides, which will further enhance their economic cooperation and the prosperity of the regional economy.

In the security arena, both sides are also further strengthening their cooperation. Above all, both sides are confronted with the common threat of international terrorism, national separatism and religious extremism, as well as drug dealing, arms smuggling and illegal immigration. Thus, they need to combine their efforts to meet the severe challenge. Further, the various bilateral cooperation mechanisms and the multilateral SCO will further guarantee their security cooperation, though they must remain cautious about the challenges of the ever-changing Central Asian situation.

- As Central Asian states face a large number of political, economic, and social problems during the transformation period, they are very likely to encounter to internal conflicts. The presidential system is the basis for the stability of Central Asian states, which largely depends on the personal authority of the president alone. Once a president loses power due to certain contingent factors, the political situation in the region may well move out of control, especially when external forces provoke conflicts between the authorities and political dissidents.

- Although Islamic extremist forces are currently well contained, they may still expand their influence in Central Asia during elections or in times of Central Asian economic depression.
- Competition among major powers, especially over Caspian energy, seriously affects the stability and development of Central Asia and complicates the relations among Central Asian states.
- Latent conflicts between Central Asian states in religion, nationality, border definition, and the distribution of resources will continue to affect the development of their relationships quite far into the future and add much uncertainty to the future development of the regional situation.

In a word, all the four above-mentioned factors might affect the development of relations between China and the Central Asian states.

Conclusion

Looking into the future, we must note that, despite the many risks and challenges, China-Central Asia relations are seeing more opportunities. Maintaining regional stability is a common pursuit of China and these states, and it is also prerequisite for the region's prosperity. With the many common interests and broad consensus, there is every reason to believe that China-Central Asia relations will develop steadily. China's foreign policy of "Friendship, Stability and Mutual Prosperity with Neighboring Countries" has been widely acknowledged by the Central Asian states and has had a positive effect. Central Asia's prosperity cannot be achieved without China, while China also needs Central Asia to sustain its own growth. Therefore, we believe that China-Central Asia relations based on friendship, equality and mutual benefit will continue to grow, bringing prosperity to both sides.

Part II

Issues and Concerns

Chapter Six

Analysis Of Relations Between Interests Of China and India In Central Asia

Yang Shu

In spite of the fact that Central Asia is composed of several moderate and small countries, this region, due to its unique geographical position and rich natural resources, has increasingly appealed to external powers, which has brought about a pluralistic power structure in the region. With the continuous discoveries of energy resources in the Caspian Sea and the anti-terrorist war in Afghanistan, Central Asia has grown to be an ever more important strategic spot in the world. China and India, both as strong regional powers, are paying closer attention to Central Asia, and their influences in this area are expanding as well, which may either lead to their cooperation on their common goals or give rise to conflicts between their different interests. This paper aims to give a brief analysis of the relationship between the interests of China and India in Central Asia.

China-India Relationship in Terms of Energy

Both China and India are giving more strategic consideration to the Central Asian energy, due to the severe energy security situation they must face. As it is generally believed, oil, an irreplaceable form of energy, has become the blood vessel of the modern economy. There are reportedly abundant energy resources, especially oil and natural gas in the Central Asian area, in which the discovered oil reserves reach 200 billion barrels, and natural gas 8 trillion cubic meters.[87] Consequently, Central Asia has become a target of competition among various external forces. Because of the common intention of India and China to cooperate in oil exploitation in Central Asia, both countries should strive to improve their cooperation and avoid opposition in the field of energy.

- **India's consideration of the energy resources in Central Asia**

Since the 1990s, the exploration of oil and natural gas in India has reached a stalemate, and no great discovery was ever made. However, the rapid development of India's economy demands a rapidly growing supply of oil, and the gap between this supply and demand is gradually growing wider.

India's demand for oil is increasing at the fastest rate in Asia, according to The Director of the Marketing Department of the International Energy Organization, who spoke at the 4th Annual Asian Oil and Natural Gas Conference held in Kuala Lumpur, Malaysia, in 2004. In 2001, India produced 640,000 barrels while consuming 1.9 million barrels per day. Its net import has reached nearly 60 million tons, with a dependent rate on oil import as high as 58 percent. It is estimated that India's oil consumption will increase from 1.9 million barrels per day in 2001 to 34 million barrels per day in 2010. Considering the current energy reserves in India, only 760 million tons of oil and less than 700 billion cubic meters of natural gas are exploitable, which can last 20 years at the most at the current speed of exploitation. India's Petroleum Minister Ram Naik Mani Shankar Aiyar revealed in a written report to the Parliament that, of the total Indian demand of 100 million tons, 70 percent depended on oil import, and that India imported 78.7 million tons of crude oil and 1 million tons of oil products between 2001 and 2002 alone, while the energy demand was still increasing. In 2001, the total Indian demand for oil was about 115 million tons, but it is expected to exceed 200 million tons in 2010, by which time India's oil self-sufficiency rate will be only 30 percent at the best. Although India's imported oil mainly comes from the nearby Gulf regions, excessive dependence on oil import from a certain area will lead to the increasing fragility of its energy security. Therefore, it is necessary for India to multiply its sources of energy supply and seek a stable and inexpensive source of oil and natural gas in Central Asia. Especially after the Iraq War, in order to avoid the threat to its oil supplies, India worked out a plan for crude-oil import in times of crises, in which India's interest in Central Asian energy rose greatly. Therefore, from the perspectives of energy and economic security, Central Asia is of great strategic significance to India, who has been expanding communication and cooperation with the oil-supplying countries in the Persian Gulf and in Central Asia as well.

- **China's demand for energy in Central Asia**

At present, China ranks third in world energy production and second in energy consumption. In 2004, it imported 122.7 million tons of crude oil, with a dependent rate on import as high as 40 percent. It is estimated that China will increase its crude-oil import by 10 to 15 million tons each year by 2010. According to relevant studies, when a country's oil import exceeds 50 million tons, its national economy will be subject to influence of the international oil market; when the oil import exceeds 100 million tons, it must take diplomatic, economic or military measures to ensure its energy security. Seen from its industrializing process, China will witness an even bigger gap between oil production and demand, thus facing a dangerous situation of energy security. According to statistics by relevant departments, about 65 percent of China's imported oil comes from the Middle East, most of which is transported through the Malacca Strait, which is famous for its crowded traffic and many pirates. To ensure safe passage for the transportation of oil and natural gas, it is wise for China to construct a pipeline and import a certain amount of oil and natural gas from Central Asia. Therefore, China should pay continuous efforts to widen the supply channels for its national strategic reserves by actively participating in the exploration and exploitation of oil and natural gas in Central Asia and the Caspian Sea.

- **Possibility of China-India cooperation in the field of energy**

The common concern between China and India over Central Asia naturally generates certain conflicts between their interests in energy exploitation in the area. However, in view of the various forces in the political realm of Central Asia, China and India should cooperate well on energy in Central Asia, especially on the construction of oil pipelines.

It can be found from a broad view of Xinjiang, Central Asia and India that, it is feasible to construct a pipeline from Kazakhstan to India via Xinjiang of China. The pipeline can first stretch to northern Xinjiang from Kazakhstan, then to southern China, and finally reach India. With regard to China's "West Gas to the East Project," whose pipeline runs from the south to the north and to the inland areas, this proposal will prove beneficial to both China and India.

More specifically, a pipeline from Kazakhstan to Xinjiang can be built first. In reality, the pipeline has already been in construction since September 2004. The agreement signed between the Kazakh Ministry of Energy and Mineral Resources, and the China Petroleum and Natural Gas Corporation on September 24, 1997, described in detail the direction of the 2,797-km pipeline with an oil-transporting capacity of 20 million tons a year, and its duration for construction was expected to be 4 years. After this pipeline is constructed, a new one is to be constructed from Zepu County of the Tarim Basin in Xinjiang to Kashmir along No. 219 National Highway, and two more pipelines to India and Pakistan respectively will be constructed.

After the completion of both pipelines, the oil and natural gas transported to inland China from the south through northern Xinjiang can be transported to Pakistan and India in exchange for the oil and gas transported to northern Xinjiang from Central Asia. To be specific, oil and gas will be transported to inland China by the two pipelines: 1) Tarim—Korla—the Turpan Basin—inland China; and 2) Kazakhstan—the Zhun'ge'er Basin—the Turpan Basin—Inland China. The pipeline to India will run from Tarim to Zepu to Kashmir, and reach India and Pakistan. This proposal not only reduces the distance of China's "West Gas to the East Project" in Xinjiang, but also provides another option of oil import for India.

From the economic perspective, this proposal can save a lot of costs, and from the political perspective, it can promote political cooperation between all relevant parties as well, especially political dialogue between China and India, as well as between India and Pakistan. Despite the comparatively smaller number of influencing factors in nationalities, religion and politics for this proposal, the terrorist forces in Kashmir will be the most threatening factor requiring the joint efforts of all participating countries.

China-India Relationship in Regional Security

In addition to the mutual demand for energy in Central Asia, China and India share a common goal of maintaining stability in the region.

Central Asia is of special strategic significance to India due to its proximity to Pakistan, a country on bad terms with India. Since the separation of the two countries,

India and Pakistan have been involved in countless conflicts over Kashmir. The vacuum of power in Central Asia after the disintegration of the Soviet Union provided an opportunity for Pakistan to obtain more strategic space than for India, who has been worried about the expanding Pakistani influence in Afghanistan as well as in parts of Central Asia since the 1980s. Particularly, India believes that Pakistan has always provided aid for terrorists in their actions in Kashmir, which seriously threatens the national security and domestic stability of India. Under these circumstances, India expects to compress the strategic space of Pakistan by developing relations with the five Central Asian states, thus preventing Pakistan from obtaining more strategic space in Central Asia and, as a further step, completing a strategic encirclement around Pakistan in some sense. Moreover, terrorist forces in South Asia and Central Asia have joined together, which requires the joint efforts of India and the Central Asian states for the cause of regional security. The instability caused by Islamic fundamentalism and cross-border terrorism is not only likely to bring about political turbulence in India, but will also impede the development of democratic institutions in Central Asia. If the Central Asian states aim to continue their secularization process, they must cooperate with India in combating Islamic fundamentalism; India must also rely largely on the Central Asian states to contain terrorism in Kashmir. As the five Central Asian states and India are all victims of Islamic fundamentalism as well as cross-border terrorism, only well-organized cooperation between both sides can strike terrorist actions effectively, especially those in the Ferghana Basin and Garm area that are intertwined with Kashmir issues.

On the one hand, in the geopolitics of Central and South Asia, the collapse of the Taliban regime deprives Pakistan of an important source of rear support, thus India has taken a more advantageous position in its confrontation with Pakistan; on the other hand, this situation impels Pakistan to turn to Central Asia for greater strategic space. Hence the increasing demands for India's security in the Indian Ocean and Central Asia. As an Indian scholar said, "In order to protect its own security interests, India still has to focus on Afghanistan and Central Asia…India needs to take necessary measures to make sure that it will not be excluded from Central Asian politics, and that it will not become a helpless bystander in an area so critical to its own security."

Besides the goal of obtaining new energy bases in Central Asia, China also intends to prevent extremist forces from disturbing its domestic stability by enhancing regional cooperation. The security of west China requires its cooperation with the Central Asian states as well as with India. Among all the international factors that are likely to influence west China, the changes and development of the states along China's northwest borders are most important. Therefore, it has become one of China's key strategic goals to maintain the stability in west China and the entire Central Asian region.

Xinjiang adjoins Central Asia geographically. The separatist and terrorist forces in Xinjiang, with aid and training from international terrorist forces headed by Al-Qaeda, pose a serious threat to the peace, security and stability of China and Central Asia. In order to combat terrorism more effectively, China has signed *The Shanghai Pact on Striking Terrorism, Separatism and Extremism* with four Central Asian states and Russia, which is an important step for China and Central Asian states in enhancing their cooperation in security.

Security and stability in northwest China and Central Asia are closely related. With diverse cultures, religions and nationalities, Central Asia is a unique and complicated region, while Xinjiang separatists in China, whose support mainly comes from Central Asia, are increasing the conflicts between different nationalities in Xinjiang. In the long run, it is both necessary and urgent for China and the Central Asian states to cooperate in striking terrorism. It is also a most pressing task for China to prevent Central-Asia-based extremist forces from threatening the stability and security of northwest China.

At present, the drug problem has become a most perilous threat to the world. Central Asia has grown to be one of the leading drug producing and transporting centers. Since the beginning of the 1990s, the amount of narcotics transported via Central Asia has increased by dozens of times. It is estimated that over 60 percent of all drugs produced in Afghanistan flow into Central Asian states, and then enter the world drug market together with drugs produced in Central Asia. Most of the drugs are transported to Europe and Russia, while some are sold to India and Pakistan, causing great harm to the local society. According to an official of the U.N. Anti-Drug Organization who is working in Russia, more than 30 countries or areas have become drug markets, the largest of which include Colombia, Peru, Mexico, Brazil, India, China, and Russia. Apparently, cracking down on drug smuggling has become another important mission for China and Central Asia. Otherwise, illegal-drug activity will not only cause instability in Central Asian states, but will also impair the development of regional cooperation.

In a word, China and India share common security interests in striking Islamic fundamentalism and drug smuggling, as well as maintaining the regional security and stability in Central Asia. It is to be admitted that Central Asia itself is rather fragile in the face of Islamic fundamentalism, whose influence will grow with serious economic or political crises in the region, and that does not accord with the basic interests of India, China, and Central Asian states as well.

China-India Economic and Trade Relations

Historically, close economic ties existed along the route of Central Asia—Afghanistan—Pakistan—India. These ties were severed by a series of incidents that occurred in the 19th and 20th centuries. It will be of great geopolitical appeal to revitalize transportation from Central Asia to Pakistan and India. Soon after the disintegration of the Soviet Union, Pakistan realized the importance of Central Asia in geopolitics, and believed that "the window to Central Asia must be opened." Thus, India and Pakistan began to compete in Afghanistan. According to the Tajik Ministry of Economy and Trade, in order to promote regional economic cooperation between Central Asia and South Asia, the Ministers of Traffic and Trade from Afghanistan, Pakistan, Tajikistan, Turkmenistan and Uzbekistan met in early August 2003 at the headquarters of the Asian Development Bank in Manila, capital of the Philippines, and signed an agreement on usage of the "South-North Passage" that links the Central Asian states with ports in Pakistan on the basis of mutual benefits.

Meanwhile, India was highly concerned about Pakistan's intention to open the passage to Central Asia, as it might consolidate Pakistan's strategic position in geopolitics. India has always attached great importance to the Central Asian market and the regional economic cooperation between South Asia and Central Asia. Due to the frequent conflicts between India and Pakistan, however, there is little possibility for India to be economically connected with Central Asia and Russia through Pakistan and Afghanistan. Goods from India must be transported to Iran by sea first, then on to the Central Asian states. Thus, Iran is not only a gateway to Afghanistan, Central Asia and Europe for India, but it also connects Central Asia with the world market. At present, New Delhi and Teheran are joining their efforts to construct a passage that links India and the above areas via Iran.[88] Once completed, this passage will witness a reduction of transportation fees and an opening of new markets, which will not only promote trade between India and the Central Asian states, but will also overcome the negative impact on India by the new passage between Pakistan and theses states. In this process, Afghanistan will be an important gateway for India to get connected with Central Asia. India maintained close relations with the former Northern Alliance during Taliban times, and four ministers of the Afghan Interim government have visited New Delhi to discuss the issue of reconstructing Afghanistan. However, the successful construction of the passage still depends on active cooperation from the Central Asian states. As far as the Central Asian states are concerned, they are striving for economic integration within their own region, and some phased achievements have been achieved. Because of the relationship between India and the former Soviet Union, it is easier for India to participate in the economic integration of Central Asia and to establish trade relations or other joint programs with the five Central Asian states. India and Central Asia may develop their economic cooperation through joint ventures in such fields as banking, insurance, agriculture, information technology and the pharmaceutical industry. India has supplied nearly one third of the total pharmaceutical demand in Central Asia, and at an industry exposition held in Almaty in 2004, Indian companies received orders worth 28 million U.S dollars for its home products. Both of these facts indicate the great prospects for India-Central Asia economic cooperation.

From China's perspective, as northwest China shares more than 3,000 kilometers of common borders with Central Asian states, as well as many transnational ethnic groups, languages, customs and traditions, China and Central Asia have enjoyed a long history of contact. Therefore, west China's development is closely related to the five Central Asian

---

[88] Shahin, Sultan, "Who Supports Iran's Development of Nuclear Weapons in the Dark?" Asian Times (Thailand), September 1, 2003.

states. Since the 1990s, trade between China and the five states has increased more than three times, from $460 million in 1992 to $1,509 million in 2001. The abundant natural resources in Central Asia and the processing capacity in China provide a supplementary economic opportunity of for both sides. In addition, China and most Central Asian states are members of the Shanghai Cooperation Organization (SCO), which is even more beneficial to the development of their cooperation in economics and trade. Currently, Chinese goods in Asia mainly include textiles, foodstuffs, up-scale beverages, fruit and vegetables, as well as medical products and daily commodities. From 80 to 90 percent of all business between China and Central Asia is conducted via Xinjiang. In May 2004, while meeting with more than 130 business people from China and Kazakhstan, Kazakh President Nazarbayev said, "Xinjiang is one of the fastest growing areas in economic activity. In the total $3-billion trade volume between China and Kazakhstan, about $2.5 billion is done here. The impact of Xinjiang on Kazakhstan is sure to grow into the future." However, a large proportion of goods exported via Xinjiang come from Central and East China, which actually increases the costs of trade. Fortunately, the Great Development of the West in China provides more opportunities for trade between Xinjiang and Kazakhstan, which reportedly reached $1.88 billion in the first half of this year—good evidence of the importance of Central Asia to foreign trade in Xinjiang.

With the economic development of the Central Asian states, consumer power is increasing too. China should revise its low-level means of trade of the past while maintaining its current market share and stepping up the class of its goods, thus better adapting to the changed Central Asian market.

It is undeniable that, both as developing countries at similar levels of development and with similar economic structures, China and India will continue to compete over their share of the Central Asian market, especially in mid- and low-end products, thus involving themselves in certain conflicts in trade and economic activity, as well as in attracting foreign funds, investing in other countries, and engaging in diplomacy. Under this circumstance, China and India should strive to develop their own strong fields, complementing each other with their respective advantages. It is proposed that an economic community, such as a free-trade zone, be established between both countries.

Conclusion

It can be found from the above analysis that, whether from the perspective of economic interests or from regional security, the development of relations between both China and India with Central Asian states is of great importance. To be specific, India and China share common interests in combating extremist forces. Further, as cooperation in energy is key to balancing relationships between large powers and maintaining regional stability, China and India should try to find more common interests while engaging themselves more actively in energy cooperation. It must be noted that the rich energy reserves in the Central Asian states not only serve as a foundation for their economic development, but they are also a major factor that may lead to instability of the region, due to ever more intense competition and conflicts over energy. In view of that, China and India should make the best use of their geopolitical advantages and expand their cooperation in Central Asia, so as to fulfill their mutual interests in the region.

In general, India and China have their own advantages in their cooperation in Central Asia. India's advantages concentrate on its culture, religions and social system. Specifically speaking, India and Central Asia share a long history of close contacts in culture and religion; the Central Asian states all believe in Islam, while India has the largest Muslim population (120 million) in the world. These traditional cultural and religious ties provide strong ideological support for the development of their relations. In terms of a political system, India has grown to be a democratic nation, while the Central Asian states are still in the process of democratization, to which India's experience is of great referent value.

By comparison, China's advantages are mainly geopolitical and economic. China, especially Xinjiang, shares with Central Asian states extensive common borders as well as great potential for economic cooperation. In addition, China's great economic achievements have been taken as a model by Central Asian states, which provides a solid foundation for further cooperation between both sides.

Moreover, the SCO can help institutionalize China-India cooperation in Central Asia. Originating from the Shanghai 5-Nation Organization founded in 1996, the SCO is a regional multilateral organization for cooperation whose original goal was to establish mutual military trust, resolve border issues, combat extremist-terrorist forces, and maintain regional security. When Kazakh President Nazarbayev visited India in February 2002, he suggested that India join the SCO, which, he believed, would enhance the strength of the organization; Russia also publicly invited India to join the SCO. It is quite likely that India may join the SCO in the near future. In June 2005, India became an observing nation in the SCO, which will undoubtedly promote cooperation between India and the Central Asian states. However, it is not yet time for India to join the SCO at present. As for China, although it played a crucial role in the initiation of the organization, its influence in Central Asia is now far behind that of Russia and the U.S. Therefore, China should endeavor to play a more active part in Central Asian issues.

It should be pointed out that due to the special relationship between India and Russia, these two countries are most likely to form an alliance among all participating powers in the cooperation and competition in Central Asia. China should give sufficient attention to this possibility: from the positive perspective, China should strive to cooperate with both countries in various fields; from the negative perspective, it should try to prevent the countries from jointly compressing China's space for development in Central Asia.

To sum up, China-India cooperation in Central Asia is the stronger tendency, though competition in certain fields is inevitable as well. At present, Central Asia has become a spot over which various regional and global powers try to exert the greatest influence. The energy and security interests of both China and India depend on the security and stability of the area. Thus, it is the common goal of China, India and the Central Asian states to maintain the stability of Central and South Asia. As two important balancing forces on the political stage of Central Asia, China and India tend to expand their engagement in Central Asian issues gradually. Because of the cultural similarity between India and the Central Asian states, India is playing an ever more important role in balancing various political forces in the region, thus beneficial to the "balancing diplomacy" of the five Central Asian states. During the process, both China and India should adopt a "win-win" strategy, pursuing their respective national interests through cooperation and positive interaction. One thing is certain: whatever forms of competition exist in Central Asia, the stability of this region accords with the interests of every country.

Chapter Seven

The Role of Multilateral Anti-terror Mechanism in Central Asia

Pan Guang

Anti-terror Situation in the Hinterland of Eurasia Following the Iraq War

In the new surge of terrorist attacks sweeping the world following the Iraq War, the formation of the "terrorist arc belt" stretching from the Middle Eat, Central Asia, South Asia to Southeast Asia is a most disturbing development. This arc belt, which has its west end in the Middle East, goes eastward to the Caucasian region that connects the Middle East and Central Asia, and then goes further eastward and southward as well to its middle part, which is Central Asia and South Asia. The east end of the belt is Southeast Asia that has recently become a risky area of frequent terrorist acts. The terrorist organizations and activities in Central Asia, South Asia and Southeast Asia originate from, or closely relate to, the situation in the Middle East, particularly so in terms of the intellectual connections, organizational networks, approaches to activities, etc. That is why it is believed by not a few that there is now formed a high-risk terrorist arc belt of the Middle East—Central Asia—South Asia—Southeast Asia.

With the United States stranded in Iraq, its military and financial resources are moving westward to the Middle East, thus weakening the anti-terrorist capabilities in Central Asia. The security situation in Central Asia, once improved considerably, has become serious again in the wake of a new wave of terrorist attacks following the Iraq War. Afghanistan has witnessed the resurgence of the Taliban and al-Qaeda, which have, in their new offensives, not only controlled some mountainous areas bordering Pakistan and Afghanistan, but also organized several attacks involving thousands of people within Afghanistan, and masterminded a series of bombings in large cities like Kabul and Kandahar. More severely, the Uzbekistan Islamic Movement, Hizb-ut-Tahrir (the Islamic Party of Liberation) and other extreme groups have become active again, making Uzbekistan a main target of their offensives. On March 29, 2004, there occurred a suicide bombing in central Tashkent, capital of Uzbekistan, which was the first suicide bombing in Central Asia. Then on July 30, suicide bombings attacked the American and Israeli embassies in Tashkent, as well as the Uzbekistani Chief Prosecutor's Office. What is disturbing to us is that the Chinese have also come under terrorist attacks. On May 3, 2004, Chinese engineers working in the Pakistani Gwadar Port were attacked by car bombs, which left three killed and nine wounded. On June 10, 2004, a group of Afghan terrorists attacked a construction site near Kunduz where the Chinese were helping with the reconstruction, causing the death of eleven Chinese workers and the injury of four. In October 2004, two Chinese engineers were taken hostage, and one of them was finally killed in this terrorist act committed by al-Qaeda, as later confirmed by Pakistani officials.

What merits our special attention is that terrorist groups in Central Asia are now adjusting their strategies, with some resorting to new approaches and putting up new appearances. Certain groups unknown before are cropping up and expanding their organizations by enlisting members from the disadvantaged masses. The above-mentioned Hizb-ut-Tahrir is becoming very influential in Central Asia, though it was established in Jordan and Saudi Arabia in 1953. This party, which seeks to establish a pan-Islamic Caliphate, maintains close connections with al-Qaeda with its plank focused on subverting the existing order. Even though it has not been listed as a terrorist group by the Central Asian states, this organization has not been allowed to make legal registration as a political party, thus remaining in a basically underground state. Increasing its membership through philanthropic activities and pyramid-selling-like means, the party is fast winning support in Central Asia, particularly in the poverty-stricken Ferghana countryside where the unemployment rate reaches 80 percent, and it is now claimed that Hizb-ut-Tahrir has hundreds of thousands of members in Uzbekistan alone.

Developing Multilateral Anti-terror Mechanism in Central Asia: The Case of SCO

Just as the terror network in Central Asia is cross-border in nature, so also should anti-terror strategy rely on multilateral and international cooperation. Indeed, this became one of the driving forces of the "Shanghai Five"- Shanghai Cooperation Organization (SCO) process. Of course, this process had its origin in the Sino-Soviet negotiations on their border issues. Following the disintegration of the Soviet Union, the negotiations came to involve "two sides but five countries," i.e., China on the one hand and Russia, Kazakhstan, Kyrgyzstan and Tajikistan on the other, and the interactions among them finally led to the creation of a stable mechanism in Shanghai in April 1996. The early priority of the multilateral mechanism was security cooperation, which included the resolution of border problems left over from history, and the campaign against terrorism. When the border problems came to be solved, the anti-terror campaign rose to the top of the security agenda, and the mechanism became five parties. On June 15, 2001, the mechanism was upgraded to the SCO that extended its membership to Uzbekistan and expanded its cooperation beyond the security field.

The Shanghai Cooperation Organization (SCO) has increased its role in anti-terror cooperation in Central Asia in the wake of the Iraq war. This has come as a result of the policy adjustment on the part of the U.S.and the strengthening of the anti-terror function on the part of the SCO.

As the U.S.sinks further into the quagmire in Iraq, huge American military and financial resources are being diverted from Central Asia to the Middle East. The correspondent reduction of troops and equipment stationed in Central Asia makes it very difficult to face up to the stern challenges in Central Asia. The U.S.has, in this context, fine-tuned its Central Asian policies. Firstly, NATO and American allies are called upon to make greater military and financial commitments in Central Asia, and Afghanistan in particular, so as to share the burden on the US. Secondly, attempts are made to make contacts with the SCO for security and anti-terror cooperation in the hope of leveraging the SCO for "assisting" the U.S. in containing terrorism in Central Asia. There have been several different opinions on the part of the U.S.in viewing the SCO since its inception as the Shanghai Five. The first opinion identifies the SCO as a potential threat to the and believes that it should be placed under tight restrictions. The second opinion ignores the SCO, believing that the SCO, after all, will not operate properly as expected. The third opinion holds that the SCO, as a regional organization of multilateral cooperation, can become a partner of the U.S. in one way or another, and this opinion has strengthened its position since 9/11, and even more so since the Iraq war. People holding the last opinion argue that, given the fact that it cannot deal with issues in both the Middle East and

Central Asia simultaneously, the U.S. should focus on sorting out the matters in Iraq and the Middle East first. Based on this consideration, they further argue that the SCO should be encouraged and supported to play a bigger role in Central Asia, particularly in Afghanistan. It is right in this context that America and the SCO begin to explore the possibility of cooperation. It has been proposed that both sides, as the first step in their common efforts, send each other liaison officers, invite military observers from the other side to observe one's own anti-terror exercises, and promote joint research and training for anti-terrorism purposes. Some others have suggested that the SCO start cooperation with American NGOs and firms on certain specific projects regarding environmental protection and poverty reduction in order to facilitate economic development in Central Asia. As a matter of fact, there is already some basis for anti-terrorism cooperation between the SCO and America, since all the six SCO members have respectively set up some bilateral structure of anti-terror cooperation. It can well be expected that the intersecting and overlapping of these pluralistic cooperation arrangements will, through more conscious efforts, grow into a more formal structure of anti-terror cooperation between America and the SCO as a whole.

Meanwhile, the SCO has stepped up its own consolidation following 9/11 and the Iraq war, the most substantial measure being the establishment of a regional anti-terrorism mechanism, which has upgraded the level and intensity of anti-terror cooperation. The official launch of the Executive Committee of the SCO Regional Antiterrorism Structure (RATS) was obviously the most remarkable event at the SCO Tashkent summit on June 17, 2004, representing another major step taken in facilitating the security and anti-terror cooperation within the SCO framework. The recent Astana summit meeting of the Shanghai Cooperation Organization (SCO) achieved remarkable results, demonstrating that this multilateral organization is now showing a more active posture in safeguarding security and promoting economic development in the region, caring about the situation in areas around Central Asia, and participating in the world affairs.

The Astana summit meeting first of all reviewed the previous documents signed among SCO members, keeping a special interest in the implementation of the official measures taken so far. Secondly, the Astana summit took the initiative in shouldering a chief responsibility for safeguarding the security in Central Asia. The heads of state decided to increase significantly their security cooperation on the basis of the achievements made so far, including particularly these following aspects: promoting close cooperation among the diplomatic, foreign economic, law-enforcement, national defense and special-mission authorities of the member states; working out effective measures and institutions to respond collectively to those developments that threaten the regional peace, security and stability; coordinating the security-ensuring laws and regulations in the member states; cooperating in researching and developing new technologies and equipment for coping with new challenges and threats; establishing new effective structures in mass media to deal with new challenges and threats; combating the smuggling of weapons, ammunition and explosives, as well as drugs, and fighting organized transnational crime, illegal immigration and mercenary-troop activities; giving special attention to preventing terrorists from using weapons of mass destruction and their launching vehicles; taking precautionary measures against cyber-terrorism; and drafting uniform approaches and standards for monitoring financial flows relating to suspect terrorist individuals and organizations. Thirdly, the recent summit meeting stressed that security cooperation be put on the basis of comprehensive security. The heads of state pointed out, "Such common efforts should be of a comprehensive nature, and be able to assist the member states to protect effectively their territories, citizens, livelihoods and key infrastructure sectors, so that they are free from new challenges and threats, thus creating the necessary preconditions for sustainable development and poverty elimination."[2] The leaders believed that, in preventing and eliminating those various technical disasters that have become significant components of the new threats, it has become increasingly urgent to protect and further develop infrastructure, particularly the transportation infrastructure. They also believed that SCO member countries should construct multilateral structures to monitor possible disasters and their consequences, exchange information and analysis, and create the necessary legal and institutional conditions for joint recovery efforts, including promoting interoperability in terms of personnel training, agent dispatching and equipment deployment. The heads of the states also declared, "The Shanghai Cooperation Organization will make a constructive contribution to the international efforts to safeguard the land, sea, air and space security."[3] The London bombings that occurred just two days after the summit meeting testified once again to the importance of the consensus reached by the SCO leaders in Astana.

Especially conspicuous were the following words quoted from the Declaration of the Heads of the States Participating in the Shanghai Cooperation Organization: "Today, we are noticing the positive changes made in stabilizing the domestic political situation in Afghanistan. A number of SCO members provided their ground infrastructure for the temporary stationing of allied forces, as well as their territorial and air space for military transit in the interest of the anti-terror operation. Considering the completion of the active military stage of anti-terror operation in Afghanistan, SCO members believe it necessary that respective states of the anti-terror coalition set a final timeline for the temporary use of the above-mentioned infrastructure facilities and the stationing of the military forces on the territories of SCO states."[1] This is the first time the SCO has demonstrated its position to the whole world that it endorses international participation in anti-terror cooperation in Central Asia, yet at the same time, believes that Central Asian security should be chiefly the responsibility of countries in the region, notably that of SCO countries. It should be emphasized that, firstly, these remarks are not specifically targeted at the US, but more broadly at "those parties to the anti-terror alliance," i.e., all those countries and international organizations that use the infrastructure facilities of SCO countries or station their troops in SCO countries; secondly, the SCO has voiced its views and suggestions, while any final arrangements will have to be worked out through multilateral or bilateral consultations between SCO states and those relevant parties; and thirdly, issues like the military presence or use of infrastructure facilities by one SCO state in another, for example, the use of the military base in Kyrgyzstan by Russia, may be sorted out through coordination within the framework of SCO or CIS either multilaterally or bilaterally.

Afghanistan: Still A Crucial Focus

Afghanistan is still a crucial focus for anti-terrorist campaigns, primarily for the following three reasons: Firstly, Afghanistan was the first main battlefield for the war on terrorism after 9/11. If the anti-terror war in Afghanistan cannot achieve a thorough victory, terrorist groups in Afghanistan and Central Asia may stage a comeback at any time, which is obviously going to be a major setback for the anti-terror coalition. Secondly, now that the leading core of al-Qaeda is still very active between Pakistan and Afghanistan, and almost all the key figures of Central Asian terrorist groups have grown up from the Jihad in Afghanistan, Afghanistan remains the spiritual pillar of terrorism. Thirdly, the production and transaction of narcotics in Afghanistan have provided the terrorist groups in Central Asia with significant funds that support their terrorist activities.

It is worth adding that those perpetrators of the recent London bombings just emerged from the spiritual base of extremism that once nurtured the Taliban. This reminds us once again that the mountainous regions between Central Asia and South Asia remain the spiritual cradle of global terrorism.

For the moment, two things are especially pressing: firstly, assisting the Afghan government in containing drug production and transaction; and secondly, cutting off the channels whereby terrorist groups reap profits from drug transactions. As disclosed by a recent UN report, the opium and heroin production in Afghanistan makes up 87 percent of the world total. Mr. Antonio Maria Costa, Executive Director of the United Nations Office of Drugs and Crime, is quoted as saying, "Political progress has been made in Afghanistan. However, on drug issues, no progress has been made. Indeed, the situation is worsening." Apparently, without the external support, the Afghan government can hardly live up to its commitment to curbing drug production and transaction. The SCO states, as neighbors of Afghanistan, can take a host of measures within the UN framework. For the international community, the real issue at the moment is implementation. A good starting point in this regard might be providing technical assistance, exchanging information and intelligence, setting up regular structures of coordination and collaboration, and the like. Mr. Mark Steven Kirk, the U.S. Congressman, has remarked following his field investigations that al-Qaeda could reap up to $28 million annually from drug-trafficking, a large part of which could be spent on Bin Laden's flight, the salaries of his bodyguards, and the buying of warlords and chieftains in the border regions of Afghanistan and Pakistan. It is evidently a very pressing issue that relevant parties strengthen cooperation for cutting off the financial chains of terrorist organizations. The SCO can also play an important role in this regard, as shown by the fact that this was discussed by SCO and Afghan leaders during the SCO Tashkent summit meeting. The Astana summit meeting stressed that the SCO should specifically step up its participation in the international anti-drug belt built around Afghanistan in order to help with the stabilization of the socio-economic and humanitarian situation in the country.

It was also decided that the SCO security-meeting mechanism look into the execution of such cooperation agreements, and, for the deepening of the cooperation, formulate a comprehensive document on coping with such new threats and challenges as "trafficking of firearms and ammunition, explosives, toxic, harmful and radioactive substances, and mercenaries as well." It is probable that international cooperation in combating drug production and transaction may well develop into an overall cooperation endeavor for dealing with all the non-conventional security threats in Central Asia, including establishing a nuclear-free zone in Central Asia, certainly also an initiative of strategic significance in itself.

Conclusion

First, the anti-terror policy should be based on multilateral and international cooperation, rather than on unilateralism. In fact, the war on terrorism has provided us with an excellent opportunity for cooperation with the various multilateral regimes involving Central Asia. We should seize this chance to promote the spirit of international and multilateral cooperation.

Second, anti-terrorism is surely among the top priorities of the world today. However, one should never link all other problems in this world to terrorism, or even further, one should not simplify all other issues into a matter of anti-terrorism.

Third, any war on terrorism should not be waged by military means alone. Military means, while indispensable in quite a few cases, can never be a cure-all. We should also focus on the political, economic and social roots that have given rise to terrorism in the first place, and this broadened perspective reveals that, besides military means, economic, political and social measures must be taken as well for any long-term solution. If the root causes of international terrorism cannot be eradicated by comprehensive means, it is highly probable that ten or even one hundred Bin-Ladens will grow up to follow suit. This is extremely important to Islamic Central Asia, especially post-war Afghanistan.

Chapter Eight

SCO and China-India Relations in Central Asia

Zhang Guihong and Jaideep Saikia

If 9/11 and the subsequent US-led war on terror are generally deemed to be the beginning of a new alliance against terrorism, the fact that is overlooked in most quarters is that regional cooperation such as the Shanghai Cooperation Organization (SCO) had proclaimed their union against terror well before the al Qaeda-led attack on the United States. Indeed, such multilateral collaboration against terrorism cannot be said to be the result of the events of September 11, 2001 – in all probability such cooperation was perhaps discussed much earlier, in order to keep the United States from decisively entering the region. Led by the Peoples' Republic of China, the SCO has been ably addressing not only the question of terrorism but has also forged a coalition of states that have common security and economic concerns. However, criticism about the effectiveness of the SCO has been voiced in certain quarters because of the non-inclusion of important nations such as India in the coalition. Such criticism gains in degree when one considers that India is a country that has been a victim of cross-border terror for a relatively longer period than most of the present SCO members. Moreover, the reported Sino-Russian concern that it would be difficult to keep Pakistan out of the SCO were India to be admitted meets skepticism because of the recognized sponsorship of not only anti-India terror which Pakistan is providing, but also because of the Islamic republic's emergence as a fountainhead of Islamist terror in the region.

This paper is aimed at understanding both the Chinese and Indian perspective about competition and cooperation in Central Asia, as perceived by the two most important countries in Asia. It also attempts to address three conceptual questions: (1) what are China's main interests and what brand of function does China play in the SCO? (2) What are India's principal interests and goals in Central Asia and how does it perceive the SCO? And (3) what are the factors that stand behind the cooperation and competition between the two Asian giants in Central Asia?

Shanghai Cooperation Organization

The Shanghai Cooperation Organization (SCO) is an intergovernmental organization founded in Shanghai on 15 June 2001 by six nations: China, Russia, Kazakhstan, Kyrgyzstan, Tajikistan and Uzbekistan. Its member states cover an area of over 30 million square kilometers, or about three fifths of Eurasia, with a population of 1.455 billion, or about a quarter of the world's total population. As the principal architect of the SCO, China plays a leading role in its functioning, and aids the crystallization of the common interests that brought the six countries together in order to form the SCO.

The earlier incarnation of the SCO was the Shanghai Five, a mechanism that originated and grew as a result of an endeavor by China, Russia, Kazakhstan, Kyrgyzstan and Tajikistan. The primary goal of the apparatus was to strengthen confidence building and disarmament in the border regions. In 1996 and 1997, the heads of state of the five aforementioned nations met in Shanghai and Moscow respectively and signed the "Treaty on Deepening Military Trust in Border Regions and the Treaty on Reduction of Military Forces in Border Regions." Thereafter, the annual meetings became a customary practice and were held alternately in the five member states. The issues that were raised and discussed in the meeting gradually extended from building up trust in the border regions to mutually beneficial cooperation in the arena of politics, security, diplomacy, economics, trade and such other areas.

On the fifth anniversary of the Shanghai Five, which fell on 15 June 2001, the heads of state of its members and the President of Uzbekistan met in Shanghai, the birthplace of the mechanism. The convening heads of state signed a declaration admitting Uzbekistan as the sixth member of the Shanghai Five apparatus and jointly issued a "Declaration on the Establishment of the Shanghai Cooperation Organization." The document announced that for the purpose of upgrading the level of cooperation more effectively, to seize opportunities and deal with new challenges and threats, the six nations had decided to establish a Shanghai Cooperation Organization on the basis of the Shanghai Five mechanism.

In June 2002, the heads of the SCO member states met in St. Petersburg, Russia, and signed the "SCO Charter," which clearly expounded the purposes and principles of the mechanism, its organizational structure, form of operation, cooperation orientation and external relations, marking a tangible institution of this new organization within the bounds of international law.

According to the "SCO Charter" and the "Declaration on the Establishment of the SCO," the main purposes of the SCO are: (a) strengthening mutual trust and good-neighborliness and friendship among member states (b) developing their effective cooperation in political affairs, economy and trade, science and technology, culture, education, energy, transportation, environmental protection and other fields (c) working together to maintain regional peace, security and stability, and (d) promoting the creation of a new international political and economic order featuring democracy, justice and rationality. The SCO also abides by the following basic principles: (a) adherence to the purposes and principles of the "Charter of the United Nations" (b) respect for each other's independence, sovereignty and territorial integrity, non-interference in each other's internal affairs, mutual non-use or threat of use of force (c) equality among all member states (d) settlement of all questions through consultations (e) non-alignment and no directing against any other country or organization, and (f) opening to the outside world and willingness to carry out all forms of dialogues, exchanges and cooperation with other countries and relevant international or regional organizations.

The SCO stands for and acts on a new security concept secured on mutual trust, disarmament and cooperative security; a new state-to-state relationship with partnership instead of alignment at its core, and a new model of regional cooperation featuring concerted effort by countries of all sizes, and mutually beneficial cooperation. In the course of development, a "Shanghai spirit" gradually took shape, a spirit characterized by mutual trust, mutual benefit, equality, cooperation, respect for diversity and common development.

The SCO institutions consist of two parts, the meeting mechanism, and the permanent organs, as follows:

SCO institutions

Institutions	Main functions
The Meeting Mechanism	
Council of Heads of State	* To identify priority areas and give basic directions to SCO activities * To determine matters of principle concerning SCO internal set-up and operation * To decide on matters of principle of SCO cooperation with other countries and international organizations * To study pressing international issues
Council of Heads of Government	* To adopt SCO budgets * To study and determine the principal matters of cooperation in specific areas within the SCO framework, especially in the economic field
Council of Ministers of Foreign Affairs	* To study and resolve major issues of current SCO activities, including preparing for the meeting of the Council of Heads of State, implementing SCO decisions, and holding consultations on international issues
Conference of Heads of Agencies	* To study and resolve specific questions of cooperation in specialized areas, such as law enforcement, defense, the economy, commerce, transportation and culture as well as heads of law-enforcement, security, emergency and disaster-relief.
Council of National Coordinators	* To coordinate and manage SCO routine activities.
The Permanent Organs	
Secretariat	The SCO's standing executive body is based in Beijing * To provide organizational and technical support for SCO activities * To participate in the study and implementation of SCO documents * To put forward suggestions for SCO annual budget making
Regional Anti-Terrorism Structure (RATS)	SCO permanent organ is based in Tashkent * To coordinate SCO member activities against terrorism, separatism and extremism.

At present, SCO cooperation has covered wide-ranging areas such as security, the economy, transportation, culture, disaster relief and law enforcement, with security and economic cooperation being the priorities, which has been widely acknowledged as a new model of regional cooperation.[89]

---

[89] On 17-18 August 2004, China Institute for International Strategic Studies (CIISS) and Konrad Adenauer Foundation (KAF) co-sponsored an international academic symposium themed "Shanghai Cooperation Organization (SCO): A New Model of Regional Cooperation" in Beijing, China. More than 50 participants including research fellows, diplomats and experts from nine countries of both member states (China, Russia, Kazakhstan, Kyrgyzstan, Uzbekistan, Tajikistan) and non-member states (Mongolia, Germany, South Korea), attended the symposium. For more detail, see "International Academic Symposium on SCO Jointly sponsored by CIISS and KAF," in *International Strategic Studies* (Beijing), No.4, October 2004, pp. 82-86.

China's interests

The most important consideration the Peoples' Republic of China had for taking the lead in establishing the SCO was security. As the deputy director of the Central Asia-Caucasus Institute of the Paul H. Nitze School of Advanced Studies, Johns Hopkins University, states, "China is aiming for the long haul." Writing about China's Central Asian interests, he writes, "While the collapse of the USSR has added an element of unease for Beijing–in the light of the threat to the security of China's borders–it also provided notable opportunities. The two most significant developments were the removal of control over the region exercised by a hostile power, the USSR; and increasing Chinese access to the natural resources of Central Asia. China has been worried about the region opening up to international presence and the increasing activities of the United States and the NATO in Central Asia, including the Partnership for Peace exercises in Kazakhstan in 1997. These worries, as well as an increasing realization of a common interest with Moscow to minimize Western influence in Central Asia, led China to take the lead in transforming the Shanghai 5 group."[90] According to a Chinese scholar, this interest can be categorized into three stages: a) protecting the territorial integrity and national unity of China, b) combating transnational crime and stabilizing the northwest of China, and c) safeguarding border security.[91]

The major threat to the national unity and territorial integrity of China comes from separatist activities represented by the "Taiwan Independent Force" in the east and the "Eastern Turkistan Movement" in the northwest. Since the national separatist activities in the Xinjiang Autonomous Region (XAR) are closely connected with the region, China finds it necessary to counter the "Eastern Turkistan Movement" through

---

[90] Svante E Cornell, "Regional Politics in Central Asia: The Changing Roles of Iran, Turkey, Pakistan and China," in Indranil Banerjie ed *India and Central Asia*, United Kingdom: Brunel Academic Publishers, 2004, p. 170.

[91] Zhao Huasheng, "Security Building in Central Asia and the Shanghai Cooperation Organization," in Tabata, Shinichiro & Iwashita, Akihiro (eds.), *Slavic Eurasia's Integration into the World Economy and Community,* Sapporo: Slavic Research Center, Hokkaido University, 2004, p.293, also available online at http://src-h.slav.hokudai.ac.jp/coe21/publish/no2_ses/4-2_Zhao.pdf.

multilateral cooperation instead of unilateral action. The SCO provides the unique conduit for such cooperation.

The main challenge to the stability of China's northwest frontier is non-traditional threat, such as transnational crime, illicit drug trafficking, weapons smuggling, illegal immigration, etc. The addressing of such transnational threats, which are non-conventional in nature, necessitates the mustering of transnational and joint efforts. Political, administrative and judicial cooperation among members of the SCO has contributed considerably to reducing such transnational crime and increasing the peace and stability of the northwest region of China.

The original objective and fundamental function of the SCO was to maintain the sanctities of the borders and preserve regional stability. Indeed, the Shanghai Five mechanism had begun as a forum to resolve the boundary questions between China and the former Soviet Republics. While "The Treaty on Deepening Military Trust in Border Regions" that was signed in 1996 had focused on confidence-building measures, "The Treaty on Reduction of Military Forces in Border Regions" signed in 1997 was aimed at increasing transparency and mutual trust. Now the two treaties have become the foundation of border security. The "Shanghai Spirit" embodied in the treaties constitutes the guideline of cooperation among the members.

The SCO also indicates the growing importance of China's strategic economic interests. The fast pace of acceleration in economic growth has made oil and natural gas the principal strategic interests of China, and in 1993 China became a net oil-importing nation. It is estimated that China will import 100 million tons of oil in 2004, and this figure will be doubled by 2010. At present, half of the oil imports come from Middle East, and only 10 per cent from Central Asia and Russia. Moreover, 90 per cent of the imported oil have to be transported by ship from the Persian Gulf and the Indian Ocean, through the Straits of Malacca and South China Sea, and finally to China's coastal areas. This oil route is one of the busiest in the world, rendering it insecure. China is not a strong naval power and consequently is not in a position to safeguard its shipping lanes. In this context, the possibility of tapping the energy reserves in Central Asia means a closer and safer source of oil and gas for China. The energy reserve in Central Asia, which is said to be next only to Middle East,[92] adjoins the western region of China and the Russian energy base in Siberia. China, therefore, has a stake in protecting its economic security in this region. In addition, China's demand for diversity of energy import is in line with the Central Asian countries' interests in diversifying their oil exports. China also believes that effective security cooperation within the SCO framework may sooner or later be translated into the convenience of economic exchange with Central Asian countries.

The SCO has also been the basic channel of multilateral cooperation among China, the Central Asian countries and Russia. The emergence of the Central Asian Republics from the former Soviet Union brought not only three new neighboring countries (Kazakhstan, Kyrgyzstan and Tajikistan) for China but also newer border issues. Initially, China negotiated on the border problem with Russia and the three neighboring Central Asian Republics bilaterally. On 26 April 1996, heads of these five states met in Shanghai to discuss the security of the borders and the border areas among them. They also signed the "Treaty on Deepening Military Trust in Border Regions" and decided to continue such meetings annually. This multilateral forum was known as the Shanghai Five. Because of growing concern about increasing threats from internal and external terrorism, separatism and extremism, the Five agreed to discuss the three aspects as the main theme for the Almaty Summit of 1998. Since then, the focus of the Five has been transformed from border issues to confronting international terrorism, national separatism and religious extremism. The year 2001 witnessed not only the change of Shanghai Five from a forum to an Organization (the SCO), but also provided new impetus for the member states. Three months after the birth of the SCO, the heads of six member states signed two documents to promote trade and economic exchange. Security collaboration and economic cooperation have been the two legs of the SCO, issues from which China benefits immensely.

In general, from China's standpoint, the SCO provides a perfect political and economic mechanism. As a leading Chinese expert on Central Asia points out, "China's

[92] According to Ariel Cohen, a well-known scholar at the US-based Heritage Foundation; the region has possible deposits of 170.5 billion barrels, while gas is estimated at 15.3 trillion cubic meters. The Scottish firm, Wood Mackenzie, estimates the proven reserves at 26.01 billion barrels and 58.64 billion barrels of possible oil reserve.

cooperation with the Central Asian states in the framework of the SCO promotes the integration of the economies in the region, and resolves the common problems of defense and development. It offers broad perspectives for close collaboration between China and the Central Asian states."[93] As the chief initiator of the SCO, China's role in the mechanism is unique.

India's Interests

Indian policy towards Central Asia is to a considerable extent determined by China and Pakistan. Whereas India fought a border war with China in 1962, the remnants of which continue to determine dialogue (and growing détente) between the two countries, Pakistan has repeatedly sought to hurt Indian interests internally and in the region. With the rise of Islamist terrorism in the region, and Pakistan emerging as the main progenitor of such a movement, India is deeply convinced of the importance of the independent republics in Central Asia. As a scholar writes, "The basic underlying aim was to ensure that the heart of Asia does not turn hostile to India. Indian policy makers knew it was in their interest to see that these countries also do not end up helping hostile forces or falling prey to the ravages of militant Islam...The thought that the violence in Kashmir was becoming part of a much wider Pan-Asian pattern was extremely disturbing because it suggested that secular India was facing a much larger and widespread threat."[94]

Moreover, India's interest in Central Asia stems from the desire to ably trade and develop economic linkages with the region. However, the absence of traditional links with the republics of Central Asia has been a stumbling block. Indeed, as Indranil Banerjie writes, "The absence of significant people-to-people contacts between Indians and Central Asians during the Soviet period meant that the new relationship had to be policy- and not people-driven…The first imperative was to open diplomatic relations and

---

[93] Sun Zhuangzhi, "Economic Collaboration in Central Asian Region and the SCO," in K. Santhanam and Ramakant Dwivedi eds., *India and Central Asia: Advancing the Common Interest*. New Delhi: Anamaya Publishers, 2004, p.149.

[94] Indranil Banerjie, "Introduction," in Indranil Banerjie, ed., *India and Central Asia.*

convince the republics of the need to open missions in India. This was done fairly quickly. The second issue was how to chart a safe physical route to the region. The land routes were out, even though they were the shortest. Air links existed and were increased. But this was the expensive route. The shortest way from New Delhi to Tashkent is via Pakistan and Afghanistan. The second route is through Chinese Xinjiang. But neither of these two routes was safe. India thus exploited its growing relations with Iran to develop a land-sea corridor that could be used to connect India to Central Asia and beyond into Asiatic Russia…Indian industry is also beginning to get a piece of the action on the energy front. Central Asia's hydrocarbon resources have been much written about and touted. Some of the largest oil exploration, drilling, and pipeline projects of recent times have been signed in this region."[95] It is in this context that India seeks an energy convergence with Central Asia. After all, with energy consumption in India growing at an annual 6 percent and oil imports accounting for about 60 percent of the country's total oil consumption, the story of India's energy needs cannot be overemphasized. Indeed, if the Indian interest in Central Asia is perceived in the light of the Chinese interests, the commonalities are quite evident.

India's interest in the SCO is, therefore, a natural corollary of not only the commonality of goals with China, but also the fact that SCO member states like Kazakhstan has advocated India's membership. During a visit by the former Indian Prime Minister, Atal Behari Vajpayee, to Kazakhstan, the Kazakh President had stated, "Kazakhstan with its substantial hydrocarbon resources could become an important source of energy to India, which is expected to become one of the largest energy consumers in the world." Kazakhstan has proven oil reserves to the tune of 3 billion tons, apart from having 2 trillion cubic meter deposits of natural gas. The Kazakh leader had also pointed to India's proximity to Central Asia, as well as its international standing, exhorting that New Delhi's membership of the SCO "would add to the strength of that organization."[96] Analysts are also of the opinion that the SCO can benefit not only from India's oil consumption, but also from its experience in combating terrorism. Indeed,

---

[95] Ibid.

[96] "India asked to join Central Asian Grouping," The Hindu, 13 February 2002.

certain aspects of terrorism as have been felt by India find resonance in the Chinese experience. Writing about the matter, a strategist has written, "The problem of terrorism/religious extremism faced by China in Xinjiang has certain similarities with that faced by India in the Punjab in the past and in J&K presently. The first similarity relates to the role of some members of the diaspora in fomenting terrorism. In India, Sikh terrorism in the Punjab was initially started by some members of the Sikh diaspora in Canada, the USA, the UK and other Western countries, with the encouragement of Pakistan's Inter-Services Intelligence (ISI) and the USA's Defense Intelligence Agency (DIA) during the Nixon Administration, but it could never gather much support among the Sikh population of Punjab. This facilitated the counter-terrorism operations of the Punjab Police. On the contrary, terrorism in J&K was initially started by indigenous elements with the support of the Kashmiris in Pakistan Occupied Kashmir (POK), with very little involvement of the Kashmiri (essentially Mirpuri) diaspora in the West. In Xinjiang, the role of the Uighur diaspora in the Central Asian Republics (CARs), Saudi Arabia, Turkey and the West in fomenting terrorist violence and political destabilization has been as considerable as in the case of the Sikh diaspora in the Indian Punjab. The second similarity relates to the external causes of aggravation of the terrorist violence in Xinjiang. While the ethnic separatist elements have been the beneficiaries of sympathy and support from the US, Taiwanese and Turkish intelligence agencies, the religious fundamentalist elements have been in receipt of support from the Inter Services Intelligence (ISI) backed jihadi organizations in Pakistan, the Taliban and bin Laden's International Islamic Front For Jihad Against the USA and Israel."[97] As a matter of detail, it would be noteworthy to understand that India and China have an already established cooperative mechanism for combating terror, which has been fortified not only by statements and declarations by both the countries' leadership, but also by instituting bilateral meetings in the matter of counter-terrorism.

---

[97] B. Raman, "Counter Terrorism: India-China-Russia Cooperation," paper prepared for discussion at a non-governmental India-Russia-China tri-logue on security-related issues held at New Delhi on November 6 and 7, 2003, under the auspices of the Institute for Chinese Studies.

Indo-Chinese Cooperation in Central Asia

Central Asia attracts the attentions of major powers not only because of its geo-strategic location and rich natural resources, but because of its unique position in the global counter-terrorism campaign as well. It is important to examine the Indo-Chinese matrix in the context of counter-terrorism from the perspective of regionalism and functionalism.

Regional Perspective

There is an argument in academia that China and India as two neighboring regional powers are geopolitically poised "natural competitors." According to an American India-China hand, John Garver, "geopolitical conflict has dominated relations between India and China," and "there have been five stages of Indo-China rivalry for status and influence among the developing countries since 1949."[98] Similarly, one Indian China analyst opines, "China and India straddle a common geopolitical space across the Himalayas and South, Southwest, and Southeast Asia. This makes for strategic and geopolitical competition."[99] Ma Jiali, a well-known Chinese India expert wrote that "the prominence of India's strategic position will to a certain extent weaken China's strategic influence, particularly in the third world, and degrade China's strategic role and complicate China's strategic relations with big powers."[100]

However, when a closer look at the sub-regions are undertaken, varying situational imperatives are found in South, Southeast and Central Asia in the context of Indo-China relations.

---

[98]John W. Garver, *Protracted Contest: Sino-Indian Rivalry in the Twentieth Century*, London: Oxford University, 2001, p.5 and pp.110-111.

[99]Sujit Dutta, "China's Emerging Power and Military Role: Implications for South Asia," in Jonathan D. Pollack and Richard H. Yang eds., *In China's Shadow: Regional Perspectives on Chinese Foreign Policy and Military Development*. Santa Monica, CA: RAND, 1998, p.94.

[100]Ma Jiali, *Guanzhu Yindu: jueqi zhong de daguo* [Focus on India: Emerging Power], *Tianjing: Tianjing Renming Chubanshe* [Tianjing People's Press], 2002, p.14.

India and China constitute an inalienable part of the strategic environment in South Asia. While China is South Asia's largest neighbor, India holds a position of preeminence in the region. Although Indian scholars are increasingly of the opinion that China "has gradually moved away from its initial politico-strategic concerns to a pragmatic approach of economic engagement,"[101] policy-makers in New Delhi may continue to argue that China constitutes the most important strategic concern for India. There are three factors, among others, that egg on India's misgiving about China's intention in South Asia. First, China continues to maintain its strategic relations with Pakistan,[102] as "the strategic and security cooperation between Pakistan and China can have a negative impact on the regional security environment from India's point of view."[103] Furthermore, as an Indian strategic analyst points out, "India hopes to 'surround' Pakistan–its "immediate" adversary–and to "contain" China, its "long-term" security threat."[104] Secondly, China is said to be enlarging and deepening its security relations with smaller countries in South Asia. Third, China's possible military presence and influence in the Indian Ocean is perceived to be a challenge to New Delhi.[105] Hence, South Asia tends to be seen more from the point of view of competition rather than cooperation between India and China.

In sharp contrast to the perceived positions of both countries over South Asia, China and India have no overt territorial dispute over Tibet or in Southeast Asia. However, the region, also known as "Indochina" has come to be a natural area of competition between New Delhi and Beijing. If India is suspicious about China's intention in South Asia, then China seems concerned about India's activities in Southeast

---

[101] Swaran Singh, *China-South Asia: Issues, Equations, Policies*, New Delhi: Lancer's Books, 2003, p.12.

[102] Most Chinese think-tank leaders and strategists that Jaideep Saikia met during his tour of the Peoples' Republic of China were of the opinion that Pakistan no longer plays an important role for China, and India is increasingly becoming the more important country of the two in strategic thinking. Questioned about Chinese help to augment the Pakistani nuclear arsenal, most strategists opined that such aid has stopped.

[103] J. N. Dixit, *India's Foreign Policy 1947-2003*, New Delhi: Picus Books, 2003, p.439.

[104] Rahul Bedi, "China and the South Asia Circle," *Asia Times*, 29 April 2003.

[105] For details, see John W. Garver, *Protracted Contest: Sino-Indian Rivalry in the Twentieth Century*, London: Oxford University, 2001, Chapter 10, "The Indian Ocean in Sino-Indian Relationship."

Asia. China's concerns are not only related to its unresolved disputes in the South China Sea with some ASEAN countries, but also to the implication of India's activities in Southeast Asia, particularly in the context of Japan and Taiwan. Notwithstanding the presence of such irritants, the fact of the matter is that there are no fundamental strategic conflicts between India and China in Southeast Asia. Competition in Southeast Asia is, therefore, one that can be characterized as healthy.[106]

As part of India's strategic interest area, Central Asia is the "immediate and strategic neighborhood."[107] The importance of Central Asia for India is not only cultural and historical but also geopolitical and economic. Meanwhile, China is a rising and active factor in the new "Great Game" in Central Asia. According to two U.S. scholars, "the Chinese policy-makers see their state as a rising power globally and regionally, with an expanding menu of interests in Central Asia that demand an enhanced presence." They add, "Energy, trade, and multilateral efforts to address common security concerns dominate China's approach to the region."[108] Compared to South and Southeast Asia, China and India have more potential for cooperation and less competition in Central Asia. In addition, both India's and China's interests in Central Asia are important but limited. In other words, neither New Delhi nor Beijing has an ambition to dominate Central Asia, considering that Russia is attempting to recover its traditional influence in its "backyard" and the U.S. is seeking to expand its presence in the region. In the economic field, some scholars have predicted the possibility of a joint effort to build an "oil highway" connecting Central Asia with Western China and Northern India. Therefore, it is reasonable to say that there will be more cooperation than competition between China and India in Central Asia.

---

[106] "The healthy competition" between China and India in Southeast Asia was first proposed by former Indian Prime Minister Atal Behari Vajpayee, see *The Hindu*, and *the Indian Express*, 9 November 2002.

[107] "India and Central Asia in the Emerging Security Environment," speech delivered by Indian (former) External Affairs Minister Yashwant Sinha at the third India-Central Asia Regional Conference in Tashkent during November 6-8, 2003, in K. Santhanam and Ramakant Dwivedi eds., *India and Central Asia: Advancing the Common Interest*, New Delhi: Anamaya Publishers, 2004, p.7.

[108] Kathleen Collins and William C. Wohlforth, "Central Asia: Defying the 'Great Game' Expectations," in K. Santhanam and Ramakant Dwivedi , eds., *India and Central Asia: Advancing the Common Interest.* New Delhi: Anamaya Publishers, 2004, p.40.

Functional Perspective

As the new model for regional cooperation, the SCO has achieved credible results in functional cooperation in both the security and economic arenas. SCO security cooperation focuses on counter-terrorism, separatism and extremism. The SCO was among the first international organizations to advocate explicitly the fight against the aforesaid three forces. On 15 June 2001, the day when the SCO was founded, the "Shanghai Convention Against Terrorism, Separatism and Extremism" was signed, clearly defining for the first time terrorism, separatism and extremism. It outlined specific directions, modalities and principles of the concerted fight against the triple menace, thus helping to lay a solid legal foundation for SCO security cooperation. At the June 2002 St. Petersburg Summit, the "Agreement of the SCO Member States on Counter-Terrorism Regional Structure" was signed. China and Kyrgyzstan conducted a bilateral joint anti-terrorism military exercise within the SCO framework in October 2002, and the SCO member states held a successful multilateral joint anti-terrorism military maneuver in August 2003. At the conclusion of the annual summit held in Tashkent on 17 June 2004, the leaders signed a document titled the Tashkent Declaration. The declaration summarized the outcome of the SCO's work since it was set up, evaluated the activities of the organization's agencies, and set new goals. They also signed agreements on cooperation in fighting drug trafficking and on the protection of secret information in the framework of the SCO anti-terrorist agency.

There are common interests and similar attitudes with regard to Central Asian security. Both China and India face the threat from terrorism, separatism and extremism. According to the "Patterns of Global Terrorism" released by U.S. Department of State on 29 April 2004, India suffered more "significant terrorist incidents" than any other country in 2003. In the time of the globalization of terror, this kind of threat has cross-border linkages. For example, reports indicate that the Eastern Turkistan terrorists, the main threat to China's Xinjiang Autonomous Region, intend to infiltrate from West and Central Asia into South Asia. It is also reported that these terrorists may establish bases on the Indian Subcontinent and attack Chinese diplomats and citizens in South Asian countries. This would constitute a new factor of instability in India, which continues to reel from protracted insurgencies and terrorism in Kashmir and the Northeast. Moreover, unlike the dual standards that characterize, for instance, U.S. and western perception of terrorism, India and China are of the view that "there is no difference between so-called good and bad terrorists."

However, the Central Asian issue between the two giants is not entirely without difference. Indeed, some of these can be spelled out in the following manner: (a) while China focuses on multilateral cooperation in Central Asia, India devotes more attention to bilateral cooperation with Central Asian countries; a press report on 30 September 2004 indicated that India plans to have its first-ever military base on foreign soil, an air base located near the Tajik capital of Dushanbe, which is to be ready by the end of 2004; (b) China has more concerns about the U.S. military presence in Central Asia. India, in contrast, is willing to have a security relationship with the U.S. and will not seriously oppose the U.S. presence in Central Asia. Such concerns about Indian proximity to the U.S. could to some extent affect ties between India and China. In this context, it would be pertinent to note that many Chinese scholars, who Jaideep Saikia met during his visit to China, had expressed their concern over the joint Indo-U.S. military exercises that are being conducted.

Economic cooperation is a key and relatively new area of cooperation for the SCO and serves as the material foundation and guarantee for SCO's smooth development. The heads of government of the six member states held the first meeting in Almaty on 14 September 2001 to discuss regional economic cooperation and signed the "Memorandum Between the Governments of the Member States of the Shanghai Cooperation Organization on the Basic Objectives and Orientation of Regional Economic Cooperation and the Launching of a Process of Trade and Investment Facilitation." The year 2002 saw the establishment of mechanisms for economic activity and trade, as well as transportation ministerial meetings, as initial attempts to explore avenues of substantive cooperation in trade, investment, transportation, energy and other areas. The SCO heads of government met in Beijing for a second time on 23 September 2003 and adopted a plan for multilateral economic and trade cooperation of the SCO member states, in which priority areas, main tasks and implementation mechanisms of economic-trade cooperation between the six SCO member states were identified. *The Tashkent Declaration*, signed by the top leaders of the SCO member states in Tashkent on May 17, 2004, expanded the scope of the SCO to issues concerning economic cooperation, poverty eradication and trade. To this end, the SCO members established five specialized working groups to deal with e-commerce, customs, investment promotion and so on. An agreement on the measures to bolster trade in the region and formulate legislation that supports the free flow of goods, capital, services and technology was also part of the SCO's agenda. All these imply that the SCO will move into a new stage of its development.

As two rising economies, China and India need more imported oil and gas to meet their rapid economic growth and social development, which could be translated into both cooperation and competition between them in Central Asia. In sum, as both China and India are set to increase their influence in Central Asia, it is time for New Delhi and Beijing to factor in the other side in their Central Asia policies.

Conclusion

Even as India's and China's Central Asian policies grow to include newer aspects of cooperation, the question that remains to be understood is once again the membership of India in the SCO. Several factors may complicate India's entry to the SCO at this stage. First, the focus of the SCO in the near future is most likely to be to strengthen its internal institution and cooperation and not to enlarge its membership. Secondly (as was elucidated at the beginning of the paper), it seems that there are nay-sayers in China and Russia who are of the opinion that SCO membership is not necessary for India at this point of time. The question is also asked whether it is India or Pakistan that should be first considered. Unfortunately, this dilemma continues to rule sundry opinion in China and Russia, even though Pakistan is a known promoter of terrorism in the region. Thirdly, while some Indian officials and scholars have expressed India's interest in joining the SCO at one time or another, others, however, are of the opinion that since "the US-led war against terrorism has completely demolished the relevance of the SCO," and "the focus now appeared to have shifted from fighting Islamic fundamentalism to that of dealing with the U.S. presence in Central Asia,"[109] it is not wise to join the SCO at this juncture. The Indian position vis-à-vis the SCO seems to have turned from one of "eagerness" to one of "watchful waiting." Be that as it may, the time has come for the strategic community in India to realize that Indian membership in the SCO would only entail greater cooperation and participation with the member nations, most of whom have to be at any rate cultivated by India in order to ensure its security and economic needs. Indeed, these can be better served as a result of the multilateral confluence that can be engineered in the SCO. The official Indian position for membership in the SCO, on the other hand, would find more enthusiasm were sundry opinion in China and Russia to cease equating Pakistan with India. History has clearly testified that whereas India is a nation that is committed to peace and harmony, Pakistan stands with states that are not only opposed to such ideals, but have determinedly sought – time and again – to promote terror, the combating of which is an avowed goal of the Shanghai Cooperation Organization.

[109] Ibid., pp.350-351.

Chapter Nine

Competition for Caspian Energy Development and Its Relationship With China

Yu Jianhua

Since ancient times, various forces have coveted Central Asia, located at the hinterland of Eurasia, as a bridge between Southeast Europe, the Middle East and the Far East, as well as between North Asia and South Asia. Britain and Russia started their "great games" over Central Asia, Iran and Afghanistan at the turn of the 20th Century. The famous British geopolitician Mackinder pointed out that Central Asia is the "world island"—heartland of Eurasia, and he asserted, "whoever seizes the heartland will control the world island; whoever controls the world island will be the master of the world."[110] A century later, with the disintegration of the Soviet Union, Central Asia once again becomes a "vacuum" for many global and regional powers, especially along the Caspian ring with abundant oil and natural gas resources. On the basis of an analysis of the factors for the persistent competition over energy in the Caspian area during the past decades, this paper aims to explore the new development of international competition in the area at the beginning of the new century, especially since 9/11.

Intense International Competition over Caspian Energy Resources

Since the disintegration of the Soviet Union, Central Asia has witnessed intense competition among major powers of the world, not only because of its strategic position in the world, especially in Eurasia, but also because of its rich oil and natural gas resources in the Caspian Sea.

The Caspian Sea, with a total area of 390,000 km^2, is the largest inland basin in the world. Its rich resources played an important role in Soviet economy. Before oil was found in the Middle East, this area had been a major supplier in the world oil market: as early as 1901, the output of crude oil in the Caspian region reached 11 million tons, 50

[110] Halford John Mackinder, *Geographical Links from a Historical Perspective*, Commercial Press, 1985, p. 13.

percent of the total output of the world; the Caspian sea constituted 30 percent of the world trade in oil; in 1940, the output in Azerbaijan alone was 22.5 million tons, 71 percent of the total in the Soviet Union, and Baku was thus named the "City of Oil." After WWII, however, the oil output in this area began to decline, and it was only 11.7 million tons at the disintegration of the Soviet Union.[111] Since the independence of the Central Asian and Caucasian states from the former Soviet Union, thanks to significant foreign funds, exploration of oil and natural gas in this area has produced quite stimulating results; this area is considered the third largest energy base in the world, only after the Persian Gulf and Siberia: the total prospective oil reserve approaches 16 percent of the world, and the prospective natural gas reserve reaches 21 trillion cubic meters, 35 percent of the world reserve. Energy reserves in the Caspian area are mainly located along the seacoasts of Kazakhstan, Azerbaijan and Turkmenistan, as well as Russia and Iran; Uzbekistan is also rich in oil and natural gas, especially the latter. Therefore, the Caspian Sea was once called "the Second Persian Gulf" or "the Middle East in the 21st Century."

From the beginning of the 1990s, large-scale energy exploration has been conducted by various global and regional powers, as well as local oil-producing states. Many famous international oil companies have established offices in the area, signed agreements with relevant states on joint exploration of energy, and helped design routes for oil and natural gas exportation. Instead of weakening with the advent of the new century, global competition over energy in the area is developing into a new stage after 9/11, as well as the subsequent Afghanistan War and Iraq War.

Why, then is this competition lasting till today, and still intensifying? The author believes the answer lies in the following factors:

- The widening gap between the sharp increase of global demand for oil and the supplies thereof.

Energy is the foundation for economic development in all countries. In the global structure of energy consumption in 2003, oil constituted a leading 37 percent, followed

[111] Shu Yang and Wang Jingguo, "The Caspian Oil and Energy for China," *Journal of Lanzhou University* (Social Sciences), 2001, Vol. 4.

by gas energy (24 percent), coal (26 percent), hydroelectric power (7 percent), and nuclear energy (6 percent). For the three leading energy-consuming regions, namely North America, Europe and the Asia-Pacific region, oil accounts for 40 percent and 32 percent of all non-recyclable energy consumed in North America and Europe respectively, and gas, 25 percent and 31 percent; only in the Asia-Pacific region does the consumption of coal (45 percent) exceed that of oil (32 percent) and gas (10 percent)[112]. Undoubtedly, oil is the major form of energy for today's world. Although the total amount of world oil and natural gas resources can meet the basic long-term global demand, the regional imbalance between demand and supply is increasing sharply. Within the "heart zone of global oil and natural gas" that stretches from North Africa to the Persian Gulf, and to the former Soviet Union, oil reserves in the Persian Gulf alone constitute 2/3 of all explored world reserves, 1/3 of the total output, and 2/3 of total sales. However, the Caspian region, with its rich oil reserves and huge potential for oil export, has become the second largest base of energy for all major powers in the world in consideration of their energy security and the diverse channels of oil import. Meanwhile, the oil-producing Caspian states have begun to pursue an economic development strategy based on their oil and natural gas reserves.

- The worrisome security situation in the Middle East.

Although the five bloody Middle East Wars between Israel and the Arabian world have long become history after the Cold War, the Middle East remains a most turbulent spot on the map of the world: the peace-regaining process in the Middle East has been in a stalemate since Sharon became Prime Minister, and Pakistan-Israel relations are backsliding once in a while; anti-U.S. and anti-Israel terrorist attacks by Islamic extremist forces continue; though the U.S. won the Afghanistan War and the Iraq War after 9/11, the anti-U.S. tides in the Islamic world in the Middle East are even higher due to U.S. hegemonic actions, such as dramatizing the "clash of civilizations," demonizing the Islamic civilization, "preemptive" military actions, and the "democratic reforms" pushed forth in the Middle East; Iraq remains a dangerous place after the Saddam regime was overthrown; the Iran nuclear crisis remains a threat to the security of the Persian Gulf.

---

[112] Statistics done by the end of 2003, *British Petroleum 2004 Statistical Review of World Energy*, 2004.

Therefore, compared with the Middle East and the Persian Gulf that are "always in the center of storm," Central Asia is naturally a better choice for energy exploitation.

- Geopolitical competition among major powers in Eurasia after 9/11.

The demise of the Cold War witnessed a world structure of "one superpower plus many strong powers." As Eurasia is a key target for the U.S. on its way to world leadership, the U.S. takes all efforts to avoid a rival that can challenge its position while preventing the formation of any allies against it. Therefore, the U.S. has to keep the initiative on the European-Asian chessboard where France, Germany, Russia, China and India are five geopolitical rivals, while Ukraine, Azerbaijan, Korea, Turkey and Iran are five strategic points.[113] This idea by Brzezinski not only guided the U.S.'s strategy in Europe and Asia during the Clinton years, including the strategy for competition over Caspian energy, but it has also been developed even further by the Bush administration. Under the favorable international conditions after 9/11, through the Afghanistan War at the end of 2001 and the Iraq War in spring 2003, the U.S. has not only realized its long-dreamed military existence in Central Asia and fostered pro-American regimes in the two countries, but also obtained a more favorable position in clearing the European-Asian strategic passage and controlling the Persian Gulf and the Caspian Sea—the two biggest energy bases in the world. In consideration of their own strategic goals and energy security, other global or regional powers are also joining in this international geopolitical and economic game in this crucial spot of Eurasia.

- The skyrocketing international oil price.

All through the 1990s, the international oil price basically remained between $12 and $25 a barrel, except during the Persian Gulf War in 1991. At the end of 1999, the price oil began to increase rapidly to $31.8 a barrel on March 1, 2000. Although it dropped again due to the worldwide economic depression after 9/11, it rose again after the 2003 Iraq War. On October 18, 2004, the international futures price of crude oil reached a height of $55 a barrel, and the Brunt average price of crude oil was $38.27 per barrel in

[113] Zbigniew Brzezinski, *The Grand Chessboard: American Primacy and Its Geostrategic Imperatives*, Shanghai People's Press, 1998

2004. On April 5, 2005, the futures price of clean crude oil for September on the New York Commodity Exchange reached $60.65 per barrel, a new record over the past two decades. If it is correct that the relatively low oil price in the 1990s was the major restricting factor for the exploitation of Caspian energy at the time, then the skyrocketing oil price in the past several years was undoubtedly a strong market force behind the new international competition over Caspian energy.

- Development of knowledge about the potential energy reserves in the Caspian Sea.

Even though estimates for oil and gas reserves differ sharply between various countries, due to the incomplete exploration of the oil and natural gas reserves on the Caspian seabed and on surrounding lands, an international consensus is being reached. It can be found from the following chart that the confirmed oil and natural gas reserve rate in the Caspian region is still very low, especially for oil, which is only about 10 percent, compared to the 40 to 60 percent of confirmed rate in well-explored areas in the world. This indicates that although the Caspian region can hardly become "the Second Persian Gulf," it still has huge potential for new discoveries of large or super-large oil fields. A good example is the discovery of the Kashaghan Field in the northeast Caspian Sea in Kazakhstan in July 2000, whose oil reserves are as high as 7 billion tons, not to mention the rather small population of the area and the limited energy-consuming market, which means most oil and natural gas can be exported. All these factors naturally lead to the promotion of the strategic position of the Caspian region and the intensification of international competition over its resources.

Fig. 1 Data of Oil and Natural Gas Resources in the Caspian Region

Countries	Oil (in million tons)			Natural Gas (in 100 million cubic meters)		
	Confirmed Reserves	Potential Reserves	Total Reserves	Confirmed Reserves	Potential Reserves	Total Reserves
Kazakhstan	736.56	12,548.80	13,285.36	18,406.05	24,918.96	43,325.01
Turkmenistan	8.184	10,912.00	10,993.84	28,600.17	45,024.03	73,624.2
Azerbaijan	163.68	4,364.80	4,528.48	1,245.948	9,910.95	11,156.898
Russia	368.28	1,909.60	2,277.88	——	——	——
Iran	1.364	2,046.00	2,059.64	——	3,144.87	3,144.87
Total	1,364.00	31,781.20	331,454.20	48,252.168	82,968.81	131,220.978

Notes: Data for Russia and Iran only refer to their territories along the Caspian coasts. Data originally from *American Oil and Gas Reporter*, edited by APEA (American Public Energy Agency), quoted by Xia, Jinghua, "A View on the

Competition of Pipeline Construction from the Disputes over the Exploitation of the Caspian Sea Energy," *Technology and Economy of Petroleum Chemistry*, 2004, Issue 1.

New Developments in the Competition

Due to all the above-mentioned factors, global and regional powers are competing among one another even more intensely over Caspian energy in the new millennium. Although competition is still focused on ownership, transportation rights and exploitation rights, it has taken on a new look quite different from ten years ago.

- Disputes over the partition of ownership of Caspian energy.

Despite the many bilateral and multilateral negotiations over more than 10 years, the five states around the Caspian Sea have quarreled bitterly about the ownership of the continental shelf and oil/natural gas resources on the seabed since the disintegration of the Soviet Union. The participants of the quarrel remain Russia, Kazakhstan, Turkmenistan, Azerbaijan and Iran, but their original standpoints have changed dramatically. At the beginning, supported by the U.S. and the West, the "Sea Party"—Kazakhstan and Azerbaijan, who possessed most of the Caspian energy—proposed dividing the Caspian Sea, while the "Lake Party"—Russia, Iran and Turkey—claimed that the Caspian energy is the common property of all nations around the Sea, and that any kind of energy exploitation must be based on a unanimous agreement, or at least negotiation of all the five countries. The main consideration of the "Lake Party," especially Russia and Iran, was that they possess rich oil and natural gas reserves in their countries, and that they were cautious about large-scale exploitation by Western countries headed by the U.S. Therefore, over quite a long time, they tried very hard to prevent Western petroleum companies from exploiting oil in disputed areas.

However, since the late 1990s, with regard to the cooperation between Azerbaijan and Kazakhstan with international petroleum companies, Russia has changed its stance from "non-division of the Sea" to "limited division of the Sea," and has actively facilitated negotiations between countries around the Caspian Sea. Based on the principle of "dividing the seabed and sharing the waters," Russia signed an agreement with Kazakhstan in July 1999, dividing the north Caspian seabed in the middle; two years later, they signed another agreement specifying their undersea boundaries and the division of undersea resources; in January 2001, Russia and Azerbaijan reached an agreement on their undersea boundaries; in November 2001, Azerbaijan and Kazakhstan also signed an agreement to divide their undersea resources in the middle; Iran and Turkmenistan, in comparison, insist that all parties should jointly use the Caspian resources or divide them equally among the five countries, and that all exploration should be stopped before a new coastline is decided. Recently, Turkmenistan is changing its position. On April 23, 2002, a summit conference of the five countries was held in Ashgabat, capital of Turkmenistan, on the division of Caspian oil and gas resources, which ended without any achievement due to the huge gap in their positions. [114] Since 2004, Russia has been encouraging all other countries to sign a pact on the legal status of the Caspian Sea. Nevertheless, due to the manifold interests involved and the intervention of external forces, the disputes seem able to endure for a long time. The only lesson so far is that a peaceful solution through political consultation is the most beneficial to all parties.

- Competition over the construction of pipelines for Caspian energy.

Ever since their independence in 1991, Azerbaijan, Kazakhstan and Turkmenistan, which possess most of the Caspian energy, have adopted the strategy of "development based on oil and natural gas." Because these countries are located inland, without direct access to world oil market, their choice of pipeline construction has been a key issue in the competition over the past decade: on the one hand, the countries through which the pipeline passes can charge a hefty passage fee; on the other hand, the issue is concerned with the geopolitical and strategic intentions of all involved parties.

In the past, most Caspian oil was exported through pipelines running from Baku in Azerbaijan, through Russia, to ports on the Black Sea, or from west Kazakhstan, through Russia, to ports on the Black Sea. However, due to the limited transportation capacity of the pipelines (100,000 to 160,000 barrels per day) and the high passage fee charged by Russia, these countries, as well as the international oil companies that investment in

[114] "Heads of the Five Caspian Nations Explored Resolutions to Disputes over Oil and Natural Gas Resources," the Petroleum Economy Website, 2002-04-26.

them, have begun considering different options for pipeline construction. Out of their own economic and strategic interests, various parties have been involved in a smokeless war of pipeline construction. At present, pipelines are under construction at different speeds towards the east, west, south and north, driven by the different interests of related countries.

Among all the plans, Russia most favored the "north route," which will maintain Russia's traditional influence over the Caspian Sea region and Central Asia. Thus, it has been trying to have the pipeline laid through Russian territory. On December 6, 1996, Russia and Kazakhstan signed an agreement on constructing an oil pipeline from Katinziz [Tengiz] to Novorossiisk, while maintaining the old one. Funded by the Caspian Pipeline Corporation (CPC), this project was first put into operation in October 2001. By the end of January 2005, a total of 50 million tons of oil has been transported through the new pipeline, and the transportation capacity is expected to reach 32 million tons in 2005, and 67 million tons per year in the future.

Meanwhile, the "west route" favored by the West is catching up. Despite the high cost of the Baku-Tbilisi-Ceyhan pipeline and the various obstacles set by Russia, the U.S. and other related countries started its construction in September 2002 and completed it in spring 2005, which will become the main route for the transportation of Caspian oil to the Western market. In order to break the blockade of the U.S., Iran has reached the first agreement with Kazakhstan based on an "exchange mechanism" that the Caspian states export oil to north Iran, and Iran exports the same amount of oil from the Persian Gulf. In addition, in spite of strong opposition from the U.S. and Russia, both Iran and Turkmenistan are constructing a pipeline for the transportation of natural gas. Another southern route runs from Turkmenistan to Afghanistan, Pakistan, and then to the Arabian Sea. Its construction was once halted in the shadow of civil war in Afghanistan but was resumed after the U.S. won the anti-terrorist war and helped found a pro-American regime. On May 30, 2002, with the efforts of the U.S., the countries of Turkmenistan, Afghanistan and Pakistan signed an agreement on the construction of a natural gas pipeline.

In addition, in view of the prospective East Asian energy market and for more exporting channels, Central Asian states such as Kazakhstan and Turkmenistan, as well as international oil groups, are attempting to build the "east route," a "Pan-Asia Land Bridge for Energy" to China, Japan and Korea in the Far East. In recent years, China has been actively promoting international cooperation for that purpose.

Though Caspian energy exploitation is destined to continue, problems exist with all the routes. The best option for the Central Asian states is to construct all the routes at the same time. As the U.S. petroleum analyst Simonberry pointed out, "Central Asia and the Caspian have enough oil and natural gas reserves for many pipelines. Besides, the U.S. should not attempt to control all of them, but it should work together with Europe, Japan, as well as all other Asian allies, to jointly explore energy for the future."[115]

- International competition over the Caspian energy exploitation strategy.

Although international exploitation of Caspian energy was not as active in the late 1990s as before, due to the global recession and the decline in the price of oil caused by the 1997 Financial Crisis in Asia, competition has become intense again in the new millennium, especially because of the skyrocketing oil price in the past two years, in which the U.S. and Russia are still the leading actors.

The strategic goals of the U.S. include protecting the interests of U.S. petroleum companies, making the Caspian Sea region a new supply base for U.S. energy, supporting the independent tendency of the newly independent states from Russia, and restricting Iranian influence. In order to achieve these goals, the U.S. is making every economic, political, and diplomatic effort to play a leading role in Caspian energy exploration, distribution, exploitation and exportation. With the support of the U.S. government, large American oil corporations have been very active in Caspian energy exploitation since the mid-1990s. ExxonMobil Chemical, Chevron Texaco, and other corporations have invested more than 30 billion dollars in new production facilities. Up to 2003, U.S. companies have obtained control of 16 percent of the oil and 11.4 percent of the natural gas resources; the U.S. and the U.K. together have control over 27 percent of the oil and 40 percent of the natural gas resources in the Caspian region. [116] The events of 9/11 reminded the U.S. of the strong anti-U.S. tide in the Islamic world; a big fissure also

---

[115] Weimin Wang, "A Brief Analysis of the Competition over Petroleum at the Turn of the Century," *Contemporary International Relations*, 1998, Issue 3.
[116] (Russia) *The Red Star*, September 9, 2003.

began to appear between the U.S. and the world's leading oil supplier, Saudi Arabia. Therefore, the U.S. has begun to turn to Central Asia and the Caspian Sea for a new overseas oil source. On December 13, 2001, American Assistant Secretary of State Jones emphasized that the U.S. will continue to pursue important long-term interests in three aspects: 1) preventing the expansion of terrorism; 2) helping Central Asian states in their economic and political reforms and the establishment of a legal system; and 3) ensuring safe and fair exploitation of Caspian energy.[117] Guided by such ideas, the U.S. entered Central Asia by way of the Afghanistan War in 2001, set up military bases in Iraq in 2003, and actively encouraged the "Color Revolution" in Georgia and Kyrgyzstan recently, which not only helped the U.S. establish hegemony over Caspian energy, but also linked the Middle East and Central Asia—a big step for the U.S. to control the two world energy bases.

Facing these forceful U.S. offensives, Russia is making every effort to achieve its strategic goal of "returning to Central Asia," which includes using its geopolitical advantage and traditional influence to strengthen political, economic and military cooperation with the Central Asian states, expanding Russia's share in energy exploitation, as well as ensuring Russia's control over the exportation of Caspian energy, especially in Kazakhstan, Turkmenistan and Azerbaijan. On April 10, 2003, the next day after the U.S. capture of Baghdad, the Presidents of Russia and Turkmenistan signed a 25-year agreement on trade and natural gas exploitation in Turkmenistan, as well as discussing the construction of new natural gas pipelines between both countries. In so doing, Russia also consolidated and even expanded its interests in Central Asia. Moreover, the Putin government, together with Turkmenistan, is advocating the establishment of the "Caspian 5-Nation Confederation," which aims to enhance the superiority of Russia and its allies over the global energy market and deter the U.S. and its Western allies in their energy security by forming a "Second OPEC" led by Moscow.

Japan, one of the largest energy-consuming countries, "regards oil as life," and is also joining in the competition, as it depends almost totally on imports for oil and natural

[117] A. Elizabeth Jones, "U.S.-Central Asian Cooperation," *Testimony to the Subcommittee on Central Asia and the Caucasus*, Foreign Relations Committee, U.S. Senate, 13 December 2001, p. 9.

gas, of which 81.4 percent of all its crude oil import was from Middle East in 2003.[118] In order to lower its oil dependence upon the world "powder keg"—the Far East—and achieve diversified energy sources, the Hashimoto Cabinet proposed in July 1997 a "diplomatic strategy for Eurasia" that aims at Central Asia and the Caucasus, in which the Prime Minister emphasized the vital importance of the Caspian region to Japan's diversified energy supplies, and that Japan should "promote dialogues and mutual trust with the region, and enhance cooperation for its prosperity." Later, Japan put forward a "Caspian Oil Strategy" based on "Dollar Diplomacy," by which Japan will cooperate more actively with the region in oil and natural gas exploitation, as well as pipeline and infrastructure construction. Guided by the proposal of Japanese Prime Minister Koizumi to strengthen cooperation with the Central Asian states along the "Silk Road," Japan launched a "Silk Road Energy Initiative" in July 2002, sending politicians, entrepreneurs and scholars to these sates to discuss cooperation in oil and natural gas exploitation. In August 2004, Japanese Foreign Minister Machimura visited Central Asia, starting the "Central Asia + Japan" dialogue mechanism to promote cooperation on energy;[119] in 2005, Japan is preparing to hold a Foreign-Minister-level conference with Central Asia; in addition, Kazakhstan has approved the cooperation project of Japanese petroleum corporations in the Kashaghan Oil Field. Considering Japan's actions since the Afghanistan War and the Iraq War, it is easy to find that Japan expects to win a share in the competition over the Caspian energy as an important U.S. partner in confining the influence of Russia, China and Iran in the region.

In spite of the lower degree of enthusiasm shown by the EU in this competition, it has begun to engage itself more actively in this competition. The EU supports the Caspian states' independence from Russia and their westernization reforms, not only because the Caspian region can serve as another important energy base for the European market in the 21st century, but because the EU considers the international exploitation of the Caspian energy as "a best opportunity for Europe to demonstrate its economic power

[118] Tomoko Hosoe, "Japan's Energy Policy and Energy Security," *FACTS Energy Advisory*, Issues 296, December 2004.

[119] Fengying Chen and Zhao Hongtu (Eds.), *Chessboard of Global Energy*, Current Affairs Press, 2005, pp.245-6.

and management experience, as well as to fulfill its long-term responsibilities."[120] In 1992, the U.K., France, Italy, Holland, Norway and the U.S., together with Kazakhstan, founded the "Caspian Petroleum Consortium;" Gas British participated in the exploitation of the Karachaganak Oil Field in Kazakhstan; a French company invested $700 million to construct a large natural gas processing factory in Turkmenistan; Daudale Petroleum Company of France even signed an agreement on oil exploitation with an Iranian company, regardless of the *D'Amato Law* of the U.S.; the British government encourages investment in Central Asia with a national guarantee; the EU provides many supports to the construction of the Caucasus-Black Sea-Europe pipeline. Dozens of the world's leading transnational petroleum corporations in France, Britain, Germany and Holland, etc., have invested a great deal in the exploration, exploitation, refinement, and transportation of Caspian energy, and their influence is growing gradually. Furthermore, after the Iraq War, in order to resist a U.S. monopoly over Persian Gulf energy, especially that of Iraq, such large EU powers as France, Germany and Italy are devoting greater effort to cooperation with the Central Asian states.

Besides the U.S., Russia, Japan, the EU, Iran, Turkey and Korea, the sixth largest energy-consuming country, India, is also an ever more active player in this international competition. India started its military cooperation with the Central Asian states after 9/11 with unprecedented enthusiasm. In 2002, India established its first overseas military base in Tajikistan; later, it helped to train personnel for the Kazakh Caspian Fleet; in September 2004, India consulted with Pakistan on the construction of natural gas pipelines from Iran to India via Pakistan; by the end of the same year, it reached an agreement with Russia on jointly exploiting energy in Kazakhstan; at present, India has already held a large share in two Kazakh oil fields. Meanwhile, India is actively engaged in the construction of pipelines from the Caspian region: in Kazakhstan, the India Petroleum and Natural Gas Company offered to participate in the construction of the China-Kazakhstan Pipeline;[121] in India's "Three Pan-Asia Natural Gas Pipelines Project," in addition to the "west line" from Iran to India, and the "east line" from Burma

---

[120] Aniwar Amuti and Zhang Shengwang (Eds.), *Petroleum and National Security*, Xinjiang People's Press, 2003, p.69.

[121] Yudong Tan and Zhang Kang, "Prospects of China-India Cooperation in Energy," *International Petro-economy*, 2005, Issue 2.

and Bangladesh to India, a "north line" (Turkmenistan-Afghanistan-Pakistan-India) is also being considered.

At the same time, despite the ongoing disputes over ownership of Caspian energy, the Caspian states have long since started international cooperation in energy exploitation for foreign aid and advanced techniques. In view of the intense competition of various powers in the region, the Caspian states are conducting "energy diplomacy" based on their oil and natural gas resources. Although they differ in the means and primary goals of cooperation with other countries, these states have so far shared a common intention: at first, they tried to balance Russian influence with that of the U.S., and later, balance the U.S. and Russia with "third forces" such as China, India and Japan.

Evidently, since the disintegration of the Soviet Union, Caspian energy has caused lasting international competition among various powers, in which the U.S. and Russia are leading players, though the former seems to have an edge over the latter. Both conflict and cooperation exist between the involved parties. For example, Russia no longer opposes Western investment in the Caspian region—the U.S. oil company Chevron-Texaco holds a 15 percent share in the Caspian Pipeline Group, where Russia and Kazakhstan hold most shares. As stated in a report by the Institute of Foreign Affairs at Georgetown University in November 2002, the U.S. has already realized its limited power; for common interests, it must strive for more tolerance for, and cooperation with, other major powers such as Russia, and it sometimes must restrain itself to a certain degree, to avoid acute conflicts.

Caspian Energy Exploitation and China

Undoubtedly, this trans-century international war over energy not only bears on the economic, political and diplomatic development of the Central Asian and Caspian states, but it is also influencing the geopolitical and economic competition among major powers, including China.

As the second largest energy-consuming and oil-importing country, China also faces the widening gap between oil supply and demand. International energy specialists predicted in 1998 that 1/3 of the 300 million tons of oil demand by China will depend on import in 2010, but the reality is even graver: by 2004, China's crude oil import had already reached 122.8 million tons, with a dependent rate of 41.2 percent. According to conservative estimates, in 2010 China's crude oil import will exceed 150 to 200 million tons, and in 2020 China's dependence on natural gas import will reach 25 to 40 percent.

In addition to its heavy dependence on import, China is also confronted with limited import sources and the threats to oil passage. In 2004, of China's total crude oil import, 45.4 percent came from the Middle East and 28.7 percent from Africa, both of which are turbulent areas with persistent skirmishes. Moreover, most oil transport from both areas must traverse the dangerous Malacca Strait.

In view of the strong Western control over Persian Gulf oil, China has to consider the possibility that the U.S. might deter China by threatening to cut off its oil import from the Persian Gulf in times of crises. Meanwhile, China's oil import from the Middle East will be seriously threatened if a war breaks out across the Holmes Strait, or if the Malacca Strait is blocked, not to mention times of crisis in the South China Sea or the Taiwan Strait.

Therefore, besides efforts to maintain stability and security of the Middle East and the Persian Gulf, as well as full preparation for any contingency, China should endeavor to diversify oil import channels and control the proportion of Persian Gulf oil in the total China oil import. As China is not able to build a blue-water navy in the near future that would be strong enough to protect its energy passage from Latin America and Africa, Central Asia obviously offers a more reliable inland energy base, other than that of the Far East.

In fact, China established formal relations with the Caspian states soon after their independence from the former Soviet Union, and has started communication and cooperation with them in oil and natural gas exploitation as well as pipeline construction.

In June 1997, China Petroleum and Natural Gas Company bought 60.3 percent of the shares in the Akzubin Project in Kazakhstan, which marks a good beginning of China's engagement in the international exploitation of Caspian energy; in August of the same year, Chinese companies defeated AMOK of the U.S. and other competitors in the international bidding for the second largest oil field in Kazakhstan, the New Uzine Oil Field; in 2002, Chinese companies signed contracts to invest in Turkmenistan, K&K of

Azerbaijan, and the east basin of Kazakhstan bordering the Caspian Sea; in the same year, the daily production of crude oil in China's Kazakh project exceeded 13.7 thousand tons, and 1 million tons were transported back to China; in June 2003, China and Kazakhstan renewed the Akzubin agreement, increasing China's share of the oil field to 85.6 percent; from January to June 2003, China signed many contracts with Azerbaijan and Kazakhstan; in June 2004, China Petroleum and Natural Gas Company signed an agreement with Uzbek National Petroleum and Natural Gas Corporation; in October, China and Iran signed an agreement on oil cooperation with a value as high as $70 billion; in January 2005, China Petro-chemistry Company completed the integration of the First International Petroleum that China bought from the U.S. in March 2004, and began to conduct full-scale exploration in its oil fields in Kazakhstan; on May 25, 2005, visiting Uzbek President Karimov signed an agreement with Chinese leaders on their long-term cooperation in the exploration and exploitation of Uzbek oil.

Meanwhile, with China's efforts in helping construct the "east line," the China-Kazakhstan pipeline has been completed. In 1997, China and Kazakhstan agreed to lay an oil pipeline from the Caspian Sea to Xinjiang, i.e., from the west Kazakh seaport Atlau to Du Shan Zi of Xinjiang through the Alas Mountain Pass. The western part of the project—from Atlau to Kentiyak—was funded by both countries and completed in December 2002, connected to the original Atlau-Samara (Russia) pipeline. At present, its transportation capacity is 6 million tons. Later, according to two agreements signed by both countries in June 2003 and May 2004, the construction of the Atasu-Alas Mountain Pass Pipeline started on September 28, 2004, with its completion expected in two years, with an annual transportation capacity of 10 million tons. As the last part of the 3,000-km China-Kazakhstan pipeline, the Kentiyak-Atasu pipeline is to be completed in 2011, with a transportation capacity of 20 million tons and an optimal capacity of 50 million tons in the future. Moreover, China is planning to sign more agreements with Kazakhstan, Turkmenistan and Uzbekistan on further cooperation in oil and natural gas.

Despite the many achievements in China's cooperation with the Caspian states, China is still facing many obstacles:

First, compared with the traditional Russian influence and the wealth of Western multinational oil tycoons, China's energy industry is lacking both in experience and in funds. The total capital of the three biggest Chinese oil companies—namely CNPC, CPCC, and CNOOC (China National Offshore Oil Corporation)—is less than 1/3 that of Exxon Mobil. China is also far behind international oil firms in techniques and equipment, as well as management experience.

Secondly, the environment for Caspian energy exploitation is not very favorable: the great majority of exploration and exploitation is conducted under rugged natural conditions; the Caspian states are undergoing social and economic transformation, with a fragile economic foundation, an underdeveloped infrastructure, a deficient market mechanism, persistent bureaucracy and corruption, an immature financial system, changing policies and legislation, and a poor investment environment. Besides, as these states are located far inland, transporting their energy is very costly. For example, the pipeline from the Caspian Sea to the east coast of China runs over 8,000 km, and is costing over $22 billion to build, the funding of which is difficult for both China and Kazakhstan. What's worse, the construction of the pipeline and the future transportation of energy are subject to the influence of ethnic conflicts and territorial disputes in the transit areas, the unstable Chechen and Afghanistan situations, the "three forces" (terrorism, extremism and separatism), as well as various forms of regional instability and transnational crime.

Third, China's active engagement in the Caspian region has aroused the attention and opposition of the West. A good example is that in March 2003, despite CNOOC's agreement with British Gas International Corporation, a subsidiary corporation of British Gas, to purchase 8.33 percent of the stock of the Kashaghan Oil Field owned by BG, the eight shareholders, including Royal Dutch/Shell of Holland, Exxon-Mobil of the U.S. and Dodale of France, decided to exercise their purchasing priority, and notified China in May of the cancellation of its agreement with BG. Obviously, some Western forces reject China's engagement in Caspian energy exploitation and try all possible means to prevent China's rapid economic growth.

As the Caspian region will prove crucial to China's strategy of diversified oil and natural gas import sources, China must have a clear knowledge of its advantages and disadvantages, seize opportunities and rise to the challenge. Specific measures are as follows:

- Maintain a long-range view on Caspian energy.

Although the Caspian region is hardly a "Second Middle East" according to existing data, it is by all means an important energy base for the future world. The cooperation between China and Central Asian states is based on mutual benefits and out of their own willingness. Despite the limited short-term benefits from the cooperation due to the above-mentioned obstacles, China must keep a long-term perspective on its cooperation with the Central Asian states and regard this region as its strategic focus for diversified energy sources.

- Develop cooperation steadily and gradually.

Because China has just started its engagement in the exploitation of Caspian energy, it lacks the necessary funds, techniques and experience, as well as domestic accommodations. Therefore, China should participate actively in the all-round cooperation in the exploitation, processing and transportation of Caspian energy on the one hand, and work out a long-term development plan, on the other. The present focus should go to cooperation with Kazakhstan on oil exploitation and pipeline construction. With the development of the Central Asian situation, China can further cooperate with Turkmenistan, Azerbaijan and Uzbekistan on energy, including natural gas exploitation and pipeline construction. In a word, only by developing gradually and steadily, can cooperation between China and Central Asia on energy avoid severe losses caused by sudden up-and-down surges.

- Work out flexible guidelines and pragmatic policies.

China should not engage itself too deeply in the disputes of the five Caspian states over the sovereignty of the Caspian Sea and ownership of energy resources. Instead, it should hold a detached attitude on the principle of promoting the political consultation of various parties. In terms of competition over pipeline construction, China should make every effort to speed up the construction of the China-Kazakhstan Pipeline, while striving to link the line to Russian oil pipelines, so that Russian oil can also be transported to China. If conditions permit, China can also consider the possibility of another land passage for oil from South Asia by joining in the construction and management of pipelines from Turkmenistan and Iran to Pakistan and India via Afghanistan. In the exploitation of Caspian energy, China should make the best use of its comparative advantages, learn from Russia's realistic policies, and abide by the international rules of market economy, participate in the international competition with fair actions. At the same time, China should also seize opportunities to cooperate with international oil firms on an equal basis. Furthermore, cooperation with the Caspian states must be based on mutual benefits, or even greater benefits for them; China's actions must accord with these states' strategy of "basing development on energy" and "development to the east."

- Consolidate the foundation for further cooperation.

First, all departments and relevant enterprises in China should cooperate with each other and provide enough funds to set a good model for further cooperation with the Caspian states; China should build domestic accommodations with the development of international cooperation on energy, and prepare various emergency plans and contingency plans for acute crises.

Second, China should make the best use of the CIO [Caspian Initiative] mechanism to develop economic and energy cooperation with other member countries, as well as coordinating and developing their cooperation in the exploitation of Caspian energy.

Finally, China should make equal efforts in promoting cooperation with the Caspian states on economic activity and on security. With regard to the transformation period of the Caspian states and the threats of the "three forces," as well as Western pressure on the promotion of the "Color revolution," China should further cooperation with these states to help stabilize the regional situation, deal well with various conflicts of interests in the region, and help these states solve their practical problems in order to promote friendship and consolidate the foundation for further cooperation.

Conclusion

The exploitation of Caspian energy has bearing on China's energy security, which is the basis for sustainable growth. Hence, China should endeavor to seek and gradually expand common interests with various parties with a more active and pragmatic attitude.

Part III

The Way Ahead

Chapter Ten

China's Policy and Image Building in Central Asia: A Perspective on Cultural Communication

Ni Jianping

China and the Central Asian nations fostered close ties through the "Silk Road" by learning from each other as early as the 2nd century BC. The traditional friendship opened a new chapter in the past decade when the two sides further developed neighborly friendship, based on equality and mutual benefit, and expanded cooperation in various fields. While China's relations with the great powers remain a cornerstone of Chinese foreign policy, the launch of the Shanghai Cooperation Organization (SCO) in June 2001 marked a new era in relations between China and the countries of Central Asia. Beijing's intensified diplomatic activity in the region was highlighted in 2004 when Chinese President Hu Jintao visited Kazakhstan as part of his first foreign trip as head of state. And the recent inclusion for the first time of three major nations in the region--India, Pakistan and Iran--as observers of the Shanghai Cooperation Organization (SCO) looks set to broaden the grouping's influence. It gave new stimulus to the development of the SCO and to further development of relations between China and the countries of the Central Asia.

Nevertheless, in Central Asia's dynamic and multi-polar strategic environment, there is a heightened potential for interstate conflict. One reason for this lies in the different ways in which state and non-state actors interpret and respond to the myriad challenges and opportunities of a much more turbulent regional context. These differences in interpretation and response are largely rooted in differences in culture, for it is culture that forms the sub-conscious set of shared meanings that guide group behaviors, perceptions and actions in the world. Understanding culture in terms of the deep, underlying assumptions and shared mindsets held by both state and non-state actors is critical for effective conflict avoidance and resolution. In this paper, the author uses the definition of culture by Geertz (1973) to describe the strategic implications of culture and cultural interplay in a changing regional context and its implications for current and future US-China relations. The author then applies the concept to analyze the limitations for China's cultural communication in Central Asia. Through this analysis, the author reveals important differences in cultural communication between China, Russia and the U.S., and argues that although the relationships among the ten states are not well developed, the concept of cultural communication is a useful analytical device. The analysis attempts to shed light on emerging patterns in international politics in the unpredictable region. A firm strengthening of China-Central Asia relations will have to be attributed to China's successful cultural cultivation of Central Asia, as well as political and economical cultivation.

Interplay Of Four Cultures In Central Asia

In a globalized world, the political abstractions known as nations are becoming increasingly irrelevant, while the symbolic systems known as cultures are continually in flux. Within the range of theorists of international communication, it is the social and cultural context in which all cross-cultural communication arises. Culture is typically defined as a symbolic system, which includes issues of perception, cognition and understanding. Culture is not merely an abstract set of folk practices, nor a collection of touristy festivals. Rather, as Geertz (1973) defines it, it is a set of symbolic systems that serves not only to define and identify the culture and social structures, but also to articulate the synthesis of two essential parts of human culture, ethos and world view. Communication theorists have long understood that culture is inherently a symbolic system, and that it is thus a close scrutiny of the nature of symbols, their transformation, and their impact that best prepares one to understand the ways in which these forces shape and alter our symbolic understandings of our lives. Moreover, it is from within this framework that we are perhaps best suited to document and analyze the salient issues of communication consumption in a cross-cultural, cross-national, wired world. The cultural influence on communication behavior is central to our field of study, and by any account, telecommunications, cyberspace, and other emerging media forms are becoming increasingly popular modes of communication. Equally, over the past decade mass media have played a very prominent role in the information and cultural communication of foreign policy as cultural industries, and communication technologies have become central to regional politics in Central Asia.

In today's Central Asia, cultural communication plays an increasingly important role in state-to-state relations. The interplay of China, Russia, the United States and the Central Asian nations will be dominated increasingly by the topic of this project: the four cultures in Central Asia. For example, Central Asians are learning English at an accelerated rate, not as an act of deference to the United States, but as a recognition of new international realities. And, over the years, the U.S. mainstream media's direct involvement in expanding the new culture of "democracy" in Central Asia is also undeniable. From this standpoint, it is not particularly useful to think of Central Asia as a politically significant region. The battlefield of international politics has shifted from the geographical and physical to the cultural and socio-economic levels. We are witnessing the contours of four cultural forces that will shape the course of history in the region for the 21st century.

The states of Central Asia may be conceived of as simply a subordinate or satellite system of Russia. Not only is this a matter of historical continuity, but also it is arguably a recognition of contemporary reality. Nevertheless, Russia's role is receding, especially on the cultural level, as well as politically and economically. This is a result of all the problems Russia faces internally, such as depopulation, social crisis and lagging industrial reform, even though Russia remains omnipresent in the region in terms of history and immediacy. Although Russia is at present relatively weak, it is the one country that not only has an abiding strategic interest in controlling Central Asia, but also the capacity to do so. During the Soviet period (from the 1920s to independence in 1991), Russian culture was highly influential. Unlike in the Baltic States of Estonia, Latvia and Lithuania--where Russians were seen as occupiers--most Central Asians viewed Russian culture as progressive compared to local culture. Here it was considered prestigious to send one's children to Russian-language schools, and in the main cities, many people spoke Russian and did not even know their native language--indeed, they often took pride in this. While the number of Russian Orthodox and Lutherans has now stabilized after the mass migration of Slavs and others of European origin out of Central Asia, the number of Protestants and Catholics, although small, continues to rise.

There is also the growing influence of American culture in particular. Western culture has now replaced Russian culture as the dominant outside influence, especially American culture. Speaking English is regarded as prestigious. Many local women, even Muslim women, dream of marrying an American or a European. Without much fanfare, exchange programs funded by the U.S. government are starting to have a tangible impact on civil society development in Central Asia. Since 1991, there has been significant growth in educational exchanges between the United States and the countries of the former Soviet Union, roughly 55,000 exchange students. Participants in exchanges range from high-school students to post-graduate professionals. Perhaps the most prominent government-funded exchange is the Department of State's Fulbright Program. But other less publicized initiatives, such as the Future Leaders Exchange (or FLEX) and the Community Connections Programs, are also flourishing. Established in 1993 under the Freedom Support Act, FLEX focuses on bringing high-school-age students to the United States and having them spend an academic year with a host family. Meanwhile, the Community Connections Program of the Bureau of Educational and Cultural Affairs, offers three- to five-week professional internships for citizens of the former Soviet Union. Participants are placed with a wide variety of companies, ranging from family-run businesses to multinational corporations.

The path also goes in the other direction, but to a lesser extent: about 800 U.S. students during the current fiscal year are spending time in former Soviet states conducting research. In addition, about 2,000 Peace Corps volunteers are working in the FSU. Over time, these exchanges have strengthened the social capital of former Soviet states. In the case of Central Asia, hundreds of exchange-program alumni have returned home and established strong new social networks. There are now over 8,000 young people in the FLEX alumni association. Since 1998, the United States has launched a variety of initiatives to strengthen and expand alumni networks. For example, a group of Tajik alumni are in the process of forming an NGO called Youth for Democratic Development. Evidence of the success of the US-government exchanges comes in the form of imitation. Uzbekistan, Kazakhstan and Kyrgyzstan have all started their own exchange programs modeled on those created by the U.S. government. In Uzbekistan, for instance, several hundred students per year participate in such educational exchanges. Over the coming decades, U.S. exchanges could end up similarly influencing future generations of Central Asia's political elite. The programs' quiet success generates hope that despite Central Asia's current backsliding towards authoritarianism, the region's longer-term prospects for the expansion of political and economic pluralism remain positive.

Although Russia continues to enjoy a decisive cultural advantage in Central Asia, Islamic culture is playing increasingly significant roles in Central Asia's political and religious development. And many more traditional people are angered by the spread of Western mass culture, especially sexually explicit movies. Islam has certainly taken root in culturally diverse locales in Central Asia, but the globalized future presents a different set of challenges. As a worldview, Islam might very well provide a welcome bed of stability in a world of change (Ahmed, 1992). As a cultural practice, however, globalization has introduced tensions into Islamic societies, such as allowing youth access to vastly different worldviews, creating a tension within traditional Muslim societies. Apart from the legacy of Russian culture, most states in Central Asia are invariably under cultural pressure from their citizens' rising expectations, which tend to outpace both growth and distribution. The intensely competitive cultures more often than not assume an ethnic character with transnational ramifications. Societies under cultural stress may also be drawn toward religious fundamentalism, which too tends to spill across state and regional borders. There is abundant scope in Central Asia for developments of this sort.

Commensurate with China's rise as an economic and political power, there has also been a weak concurrent rise in China's soft power in Central Asia. China is emerging now as the most powerful and dynamic, immediate neighbor of Central Asia. Nevertheless, Chinese culture is not yet dominant in any country, or even comparable either to the Russian culture by tradition and history, or to the very visible and captivating presence of American culture. Chinese culture, cuisine, calligraphy, cinema, art, medicine and fashion fads have been weak in strengthening the region's culture. It is growing, because new routes of trade, such as pipelines, highways, and railroads are linking

Central Asia to the world and are having the effect of increasing China's involvement and physical presence, which is already quite evident when one visits the market places in major Central Asian cities. Meanwhile, China's flagship consumer brand names have not been popular in Central Asia. This branding of Chinese goods upwards in Central Asian markets will have positive soft power and imaging effects on Central Asia societies.

Overall, the American culture is in a relatively favorable position because the influence of Chinese culture in Central Asia likely will be gradual, skillfully executed, and would not precipitate conflict. Also, the Chinese culture is to "go westward" by insisting the government as a leading force encourage cultural enterprises to operate in accordance with international practices. China's cultural influence in Central Asia wanes as it moves further from China's borders. More important, the American culture has become an influencing force on par, if not greater than the Russian, due to the ongoing realities of the War on Terrorism. Thus, Chinese culture represents only one of the influences for the societies in Central Asian states, limiting Beijing's ability to play an essential or irreplaceable role in the region. And there is the lingering Chinese fear of strategic encirclement by American forces and a view that the American presence in Central Asia is inherently threatening. It would help if the U.S. would be more transparent and reach out to China as a partner in stabilizing Central Asia. The U.S.-China dialogue on terrorism can only improve the larger bilateral relationship. Overall, the American culture, by and large, is probably benefiting from the fact that instead of monolithic control over the region, it is going to have a more complicated interplay between an expanding, indirect influence of Chinese culture and a receding but less threatening Russian culture.

Limitations for China's cultural communication

Insofar as China represents only one of a number of markets and sources of capital for the Central Asian states, its ability to play a vital and irreplaceable role of culture throughout the entire region is still limited. There are certain inherent challenges against Chinese culture, as well as some disadvantages in terms of China's intercultural communication, in particular, in the region. Four major factors will constrain China's cultural influence in the Central Asian nations.

First is the lingering perception of China as a threat to the region. Over the past decade, Beijing has developed friendly relations with Central Asian neighbors Kazakhstan, Kyrgyzstan and Tajikistan, cooperating on a range of political, economic and security issues. But some Central Asians continue to see China as a potential threat to the region. These fears come despite the friendly relations that have developed between regional governments. And the Chinese government and Chinese officials are extremely worried about the perception in the wider world that China poses any kind of threat. China officially disavows any belief that it is seeking hegemony in the region and has repeatedly stressed that it wants to offer cooperation, not domination. But such assurances have not kept Central Asians from worrying about the long-term consequences of a Chinese superpower. Central Asia's fears about China are rooted both in history and concerns about future jobs and regional influence. And for some Central Asians, the SCO is a guarantee against any kind of regional threat from Beijing, though it has expanded its focus to include the fight against terrorism, extremism and separatism, as well as the promotion of economic cooperation.

The second problem concerns the limited resources China can commit to cultural communication in Central Asia. China achieves all it needs through political and economic diplomacy, but Central Asia is still not a top priority for decision makers in Beijing. China's prospects for safeguarding its cultural interests in Central Asia are well served by its current counterterrorism policy. Like language, religion has an atavistic appeal that captures the imagination of the insecure, and can become the driving force of political mobilization and power in societies striving to combine economic growth with participatory politics. It is true that the conflicts in Central Asia are largely among Muslims, but that does not diminish the power of Islam to unify specific groups against others, as is evident in Tajikistan. And this region's stronger ethnic affinity and economic orientation toward Russia also render it less susceptible to Chinese cultural domination. Therefore, many difficulties remain as to how China will approach the transnational appeal of Islam in such a way as to avoid conflicts in the region.

Different sources of regional instability, namely, separatism and the rise of fundamentalist Islam, especially when it is linked to separatist activity, as well as the terrorism, are the third factor limiting the potential growth of Chinese cultural influence in the region. Moreover, the roots of these problems still remain, even after 9/11. Imminent leadership change, as many of Central Asia's founding presidents leave their posts (by choice or not), is also a source of instability. The political stability of the Central Asian states themselves will clearly play a role in how Chinese cultural influence there evolves. It should be evident by now that these three forces have important implications at the foundational level for intercultural communication theory, namely, our very understanding of culture, society, and communication in Central Asia. Chinese counterterrorism efforts provide added weight to the SCO's role and, therefore, afford China a better opportunity to communicate its cultural interests in the region. However, China can now better pursue its policies regarding outside influence in Xinjiang by having greater attention paid to border security and the movement of Central Asian extremists.

Last, China faces the task of establishing conditions conducive to the cultural communication. These conditions include not only political and legal institutions, but also a fresh vision of how the values of traditional and modern Chinese cultures can be fused into a long-term, coherent vision of political morality that serves China's national interest. The traditional Chinese culture based on Confucianism instills in people such virtues as filial piety, fraternal love, loyalty, and sincerity, and reminds them that rights are only a last resort for protecting their interests. The traditional Chinese values seem a logical aid to help build a contemporary Chinese ethos. China is moving along this very path, and hence a conscious effort to revitalize cultural and spiritual values to counteract these challenges is both necessary and desirable. Without such an effort, these values may slowly disappear, leaving a moral vacuum to be filled only by other cultures, with their accompanying narrow and limited vocabulary. In short, we now have a new opportunity for a more accurate appreciation of the strengths and limits of the traditional Chinese culture.

Cultural communication: China's image building

Along with the international community, China is willing to renew its efforts to preserve stability and promote development in Central Asia. China's primary interest in Central Asia derives from its overall foreign-policy strategy of seeking a peaceful environment. With a continuous development of China's engagement with the European Union, the region acts as a trans-continental link, not only in a geographical sense, but also in a cultural, as well as a political sense. The Chinese government is committed to projecting itself as a peace-loving nation, and stressing that everyone in the region can benefit from China's peaceful rise.

China is burnishing its image as a cooperative player and a stabilizing force in the region. And for China, national image building through cultural communication is useful in three ways. First, it throws light on the foreign policies of China's response to a changed geopolitical landscape. Second, it enhances our knowledge of the ways in which geopolitical change affects the behavior patterns of states, for instance, the ways in which they reformulate self-images or extend competition to new arenas (India-Pakistan). Finally, the new pattern of interstate politics also emphasizes a more fundamental cultural continuity in state behavior. Clearly the cultural stuff of national image is still power and national interest and all the strategic and tactical games that go with them. And diplomatically, the Chinese are always keen to project an image of international cooperation rather than confrontation, and they're very keen to be seen as good neighbors within the region. But culturally, what China most needs to do is learn much more about cross-cultural communication in the region, and the effects of China's cultural communication still leave much room for improvement, especially compared with those of Russia and the U.S.

China's fundamental interests in the region are the basis for carrying out Chinese cultural communication. China should launch some major cultural projects in the region. These projects should be coordinated with important diplomatic and comprehensive activities, including a Chinese culture year, culture week, and culture day, and create a good cultural atmosphere. Only the convergence of China's rise in economic, political and soft power, Central Asia's softened threat perception of China, and the rise of ethnic Chinese culture in Central Asia will presage healthy future development and growth in

China-Central Asia relations. By extension, it is communication skills, both in sending and receiving, that determine how well an individual, an organization, an industry, or a nation, does in acquiring and applying knowledge, thus broadening the chances for successful cross-cultural communication. Certainly, the ability to negotiate effectively the cultural issues inherent in communication gives a more competitive edge in a globalized world.

Also, China should make greater efforts to promote cultural communication and dialogue among different civilizations, playing an increasingly greater role in international affairs. The central government should encourage and support exchanges in the fields of culture, media, academia and tourism. First, China should launch a variety of initiatives to boost high-level cultural contacts, improve the cooperation mechanism in the field, and provide support on major issues related to cultural exchanges. For example, more translations of classic Chinese works should be available in Central Asian nations, as well as an intensified cultivation of China hands in the universities and institutes in those nations, so that they help to diminish the prejudice against China prevailing among Central Asians. Second, the local Chinese embassies in Central Asia should make greater efforts to educate and take care of the local Chinese for projecting a preferred national image, since the Chinese themselves are just the vehicles of cultural communication. Third, China should make a greater investment in Chinese learning and broadcasting programs in Central Asian nations and improve pragmatic cooperation in the field of cultural exchanges, such as setting up websites for a wider coverage of the young people, so that a louder and louder China voice could be heard in the region.

Conclusion

In a geopolitically transformed region of Central Asia, new analytical frameworks can yield an improved understanding of altered strategic relationships. This paper shows that each of the four cultures in Central Asia has substantial strategic relevance for the others. This is less evident from the existing patchwork of political, economic, and other interactions among the countries in Central Asia nations. Given the significant impact of the interplay of four cultures in Central Asia, the potential for political instability, and the

Central Asian nations' current backsliding towards different cultures, cross-cultural communication in the region will remain vital for an integrated politics and for the region's longer-term prospects for the expansion of political, economic and cultural pluralism.

The author's goal in this essay has been to provide some initial probes into the role of cross-cultural communication in national image projection. Given the transforming effects of globalization and informatization in the social and cultural worlds, it is imperative for scholars of cross-cultural communication to begin to understand how these forces will affect not only the foundational theoretical assumptions of our scholarship, but also the significant impact of these trends on the actual practice of cross-cultural communication. The twin forces of globalization and informatization can perhaps be best explained from within a framework provided by cross-cultural communication theorists, as from its earliest days the discipline has been concerned with the development of global consciousness, the overcoming of the conceptual and behavioral defaults provided by culture, and how communication changes individuals, in particular the policy makers.

Central Asia today represents for China both a potential market for China's growing economy and a source of strategically important raw materials. China's strategy towards Central Asia remains to seek influence over the developing economic life of the region and to maintain political stability through mutual cooperation. Over the coming years, China will continue to engage Central Asia and exert an increasing, though limited, amount of cultural influence over the region. And the Central Asian countries are also eager to continue their cooperation with China on the principle of mutual interests.

References

1. David Easton, A Framework for Political Analysis (Englewood—Cliffs, NJ: Prentice Hall, 1965).
2. Ali Banuazizi and Myron Weiner, "Introduction," in Ali Banuazizi and Myron Weiner, eds., The New Geopolitics of Central Asia and Its Borderlands (Bloomington and Indianapolis, IN: Indiana University Press, 1994).
3. *Eurasia Insight*, "Exchange Programs Having Quiet Impact In Central Asia," by David Mikosz 3/07/01, Posted March 7, 2001, Eurasianet http://www.eurasianet.org/.
4. *Eurasia Insight*, "Central Asia: China's Mounting Influence," by Jeremy Bransten 11/23/04 A EurasiaNet Partner Post from RFE/RL, http://www.eurasianet.org/.
5. "Prospects for China's Influence in Central Asia,"<http://www.csis.org/china/030205_ce_forum01.pdf>.
6. Freeman Chair in China Studies, Event Summary, China's Emergence in Central Asia: Security, Diplomatic, and Economic Interests, Forum One: The Current State of China – Central Asia Diplomacy and Implications for U.S. Foreign Policy, Wednesday, February 5, 2003, <http://www.csis.org/china/030205_ce_forum01.pdf>
7. Shanghai group aims to keep U.S. in check, by Sergei Blagov, http://www. atimes.com .
8. Clifford Geertz, The Interpretation of Cultures: Selected Essays. New York: Basic Books, Inc., 1973.

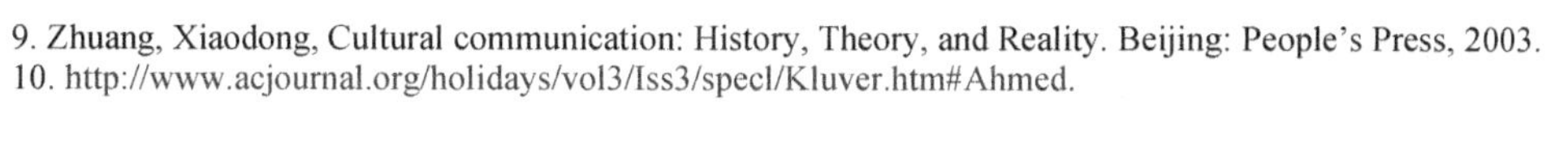

9. Zhuang, Xiaodong, Cultural communication: History, Theory, and Reality. Beijing: People's Press, 2003.
10. http://www.acjournal.org/holidays/vol3/Iss3/specl/Kluver.htm#Ahmed.

Chapter Eleven

The Common Interests of the U.S. and China, and Prospects for Cooperation

Fu Yong

The strategic position of Central Asia is increasingly important after the disintegration of the Soviet Union, arousing the continuous concern of various global and regional powers. China and the U.S., among others, share many common interests as well as conflicts in this region, which renders their relationship a mixture of cooperation and competition. However, the difference in their respective interests and order of focused issues may impede the further development of their relationship, and even impair their existing relations carefully built over the past decade. Through an analysis of the respective interests and order of focused issues of the U.S. and China in Central Asia, this paper illustrates both countries' misperceptions of the other's interests, and thus points out their common interests for better cooperation in Central Asia.

This paper is divided into three parts: the first mainly analyzes China's deepening understanding of U.S. influence in Central Asia, especially the different focal points of both countries on U.S. interests in the region, including the development of U.S.-Central Asia relations before 9/11, the U.S. military presence in Central Asia after 9/11, and the U.S.' role in the recent "color revolution" in the region; the second part of the paper analyzes the U.S. perception of China's strategic goals in Central Asia and emphasizes its different understandings of China's interests in the region, including the U.S. view on the SCO, cooperation between China and Central Asia on energy exploitation, as well as the geopolitical significance of China's peaceful rise in the region; the third part discusses both countries' common interests in Central Asia and fields for their cooperation, especially in non-traditional security and regional security, including anti-terrorism and combating transnational crime, cooperating on energy, maintaining regional stability, and avoiding conflicts between large powers. The paper also explores the possibility of U.S.-SCO cooperation and ways to establish a mechanism for U.S.-China mutual military trust, as well as other cooperation in the broad field of non-traditional security. Finally, the paper draws a brief conclusion that some conflicts between the interests of China and the U.S. are caused by misperceptions, and others by the influence of their general relationship, and that if both countries have a better understanding of each other's interests as well as their common interests in Central Asia, they can conduct better cooperation in the region, which will prove conducive both to the stability of the region and to the further development of China-U.S. relations.

China's Perception of U.S. interests in Central Asia

Central Asia lies in the hinterland of Eurasia, linking the Middle East to Eurasia. It remains a flashpoint for global powers after the Cold War, due to its geopolitical position on the map, which was described by the geopolitical analyst Mackinder as an "island of the world," with Central Asia as its "heartland." The importance of Central Asia also lies in its abundant resources of oil and natural gas. As estimated by the U.S. Department of Energy, oil reserves in the Caspian Sea are between 90 and 200 billion barrels, which accounts for 8 percent of the world's total oil reserves; natural gas reserves of the Caspian Sea comprise around 14 trillion cubic meters, 4.3 percent of the world's total reserves. Therefore, in a certain sense, whoever controls Central Asian energy is likely to dominate the 21st-century global energy market, and even to manipulate the economic development of many countries. Further, this region has become a major battlefield against international terrorism and transnational crime since 9/11 and the Afghanistan War, in which all major powers hold crucial security interests.

U.S. interests in Central Asia include the above-mentioned three aspects, namely, geopolitics, energy, and international anti-terrorism, but the order of their priority has been adjusted since 9/11 and the Afghanistan War. The U.S. interests in Central Asia from the disintegration of the Soviet Union to 9/11 focused on geopolitics and energy, reflected in the 1997 "New Central Asia Strategy," with which the U.S. changed its policy of largely ignoring the Central Asian states in the early 1990s, and began to put Central Asia into its own sphere of interest. By supporting the Central Asian states' independence from Russia and weakening Russian influence in the region, the U.S. has gradually turned the region into another place of strategic interest and to a great extent established U.S. influence in Central Asia. Meanwhile, the U.S. aims to turn the region into another energy base by encouraging U.S. companies to participate in energy exploitation, and by expanding connections with Central Asian states in politics, economic activity, and the military, among other fields. However, anti-terrorism has become the priority for the U.S. in Central Asia since 9/11, which to a great degree altered the traditional U.S. security outlook as well as its global security strategy.

China acknowledges that the U.S. holds important interests in economic activity, geopolitics and security in Central Asia, but Chinese scholars and policy-makers have different understandings of the order of U.S. strategic priorities in the region. For the U.S., the order of its focal concerns may be anti-terrorism—energy—geopolitics, while for China the order may be quite the opposite. Compared with energy and anti-terrorism, China, in consideration of the new strategic situation in Central Asia and general U.S.-China relations, is more concerned with the U.S. factor in the geopolitics of Central Asia, especially since the U.S. military force entered the region after 9/11. As the sole superpower after the Cold War, U.S.' Central Asia strategy is only part of its global strategy, which aims to maintain its victory of the Cold War and prevent any regional power or other forces from challenging U.S. supremacy, as demonstrated both by its containment of Russia and China before 9/11 and by its military attacks on international terrorism after 9/11. Therefore, China pays greatest attention to the geopolitical significance of the development of U.S.-Central Asia relations and the geopolitical influence of the U.S. military presence in the region, as well as the U.S. role in the "color revolution" of the Central Asian states.

- U.S.-Central Asia relationship before 9/11

Traditionally under the control of Russia and as the strategic backdoor neighbor of China, Central Asia is distant from the U.S. in geography, and there were few, if any, connections between the two countries in history. Yet after the Cold War, the U.S. began to show great interest in developing relations with Central Asian states, not only because of the region's rich energy resources, but more importantly, because of its important geopolitical position. The major target of U.S. containment in the region is not China, but Russia. The U.S. believes that successful control of Central Asia and the Caspian region will press on Russia's strategic space and reduce China's influence in Central Asia, as well as control the situation in Afghanistan and improve U.S. energy security. In order to achieve this goal, the U.S. has adopted many specific measures:

First of all, it helps Central Asian states overcome economic difficulties through investment, loans and grants, so as to reduce their economic dependence on Russia; further, it encourages these states to organize an economic cooperation mechanism without Russian participation, the Economic Community of Central Asia, and advocates the construction of the Baku-Ceyhan Oil Pipeline that does not pass through Russia, both aiming to attenuate Russia's control over energy exportation in Central Asia.

Second, the U.S. is exerting more influence over leaders of Central Asian states though summit visits and by signing treaties or agreements, while promoting "democratic reform" and "free economy" in these states, so as to prevent them from returning to the track of Russia.

Next, the U.S. is trying to "Americanize" the military forces in Central Asia through military aid, communication and cooperation with the region, as well as with the help of NATO. At present, all five Central Asian states are participants in NATO's "Peaceful Partnership for Peace" program; meanwhile, the U.S. continues to expand the size and area of the "Central Asian Peacekeeping Exercise" in order to strengthen its military presence and ensure its security interests in Central Asia.

In a word, the essence of the so-called "Silk Road Strategy" concerning the overall security of energy, trade, geopolitics and Central Asia, is to contain Russia and China, as well as to secure U.S. economic and strategic interests, through active engagement in the energy exploitation and cooperation with the Caucasus and Central Asia.

- U.S. military presence in Central Asia after 9/11

The priority in U.S. strategic concerns has changed over the past years. Before 9/11, the major U.S. strategic concern was China and Russia, its prospective rivals, while after the incident, international terrorism has become the biggest threat to U.S. security. With the common interests of anti-terrorism, China and Russia become partners of the U.S. in striking terrorism in Central Asia, and both support, or at least acquiesce, to the entry of U.S. troops into the region. So far, military bases in three Central Asian states have been leased to the U.S.

Despite the positive impact of the U.S. military presence on anti-terrorism in the region, its negative effect, especially after the U.S. victory in the Afghanistan anti-terrorist war, has been increasingly noticeable. Regardless of its repeated pledges to withdraw its troops from Central Asia in the shortest possible time, and the formal declaration of the SCO to call for a withdrawal deadline, the U.S. has no intention of withdrawing its troops from Central Asia in the foreseeable future. Although from the U.S. perspective, its military presence in Central Asia is not aimed at Russia or China, the geopolitics of the region has become more favorable for the U.S. with the simple fact that U.S. troops are stationed right on the Chinese and Russian borders. The U.S. has become an ever more important player on the Eurasian "chessboard" described by Brzezinski. With its security connections with Uzbekistan, Kyrgyzstan and Tajikistan, not only can the U.S. monitor and contain China and Russia more easily, but Iranian influence in Central Asia can also be downplayed. As it unfolds, the U.S. military engagement is bringing back a "zero-sum" air to the security competition in the region, and even diverting the original major security concern, striking the "three forces" of terrorism, extremism and separatism.

The U.S. military presence in Central Asia poses a great challenge, if not yet a direct threat, to the geopolitical milieu for China's development. Above all, some U.S. military bases in Central Asia are next to Xinjiang, which may threaten the security of west China; moreover, the U.S. military actions after 9/11—entering South Asia, returning to Southeast Asia, launching the Iraq War, and strengthening the U.S.s status on the Middle East issues, etc.—have begun to affect China's strategic space, whether out of the practical need for anti-terrorism or out of the goal of containing China in the long run. China worries that Central Asia, its backdoor neighbor, would become a frontline battleground if any drastic changes were to take place in China-U.S. relations. Therefore, China tends to interpret U.S. actions in Central Asia into more than simply anti-terrorist concerns, even more so with the U.S. vacillation on its Xinjiang policies. For example, on the one hand, the U.S. admits that the "East Turkistan Liberation Movement" is a terrorist organization; one the other, it continues to provide financial aid to the Uyghur

Association in America, an organization that advocates "the independence of Xinjiang," and the U.S. State Department declined China's request to extradite the Uygur prisoners in Guantanamo, with the excuse of worrying these prisoners might be maltreated or sentenced to death by China.

- The U.S. role in the "color revolution" in Central Asia

Although the recent political turbulence in Kyrgyzstan and Uzbekistan resulted mainly from their domestic political, economic and social problems, the U.S. cannot be ignored as a factor. Since the disintegration of the Soviet Union, the U.S. has been trying to transform the Central Asian states with such values as democracy, freedom and human rights, and by means of financial aid primarily. However, it will not unconditionally support the "autocratic" governments of these states, but it has been urging them to implement economic and political reform and improve the status of human rights.

After 9/11, the U.S. "peaceful transformation" policy for Central Asia has been revised, which connects the democratic development of the region with U.S. security. The U.S. believes that the autocratic regimes in Central Asia are fertile soil for the development of Islamic extremist and terrorist forces, which will in turn threaten U.S. security; to eradicate terrorism, the U.S. must make efforts to promote U.S. democracy throughout the world, while Central Asia is, for now, the key to the global democratization plan of the U.S.

China is quite apprehensive that the Central Asian situation might turn out to be unfavorable for China, as either domestic instability of the Central Asian states or regional turbulence brought about by major power competition will pose serious threats to China's security: on the one hand, the overthrow of existing governments by political dissidents with the help of external forces may engender an "expansion effect"; on the other hand, the policies of the political dissidents after they have assumed power may shake the existing security and cooperation mechanisms, thus affecting China's role in Central Asia.

Further, China is worried about the increasing uncertainty and instability in the region led by the Russia-U.S. competition behind the "color revolution." Generally speaking, during the process of the political transformation of Central Asia, Russia tends to support the existing regimes, while the U.S. tends to support political dissidents to accelerate the political transformation. However, the U.S.'s efforts have more often than not pushed some Central Asian states to turn to Russia for help, as they consider the U.S. a key factor that causes the political turbulence and instability of the region.

The U.S. Perception of China's Strategic Goals in Central Asia

As China and the U.S. differ greatly in the focus of strategic concerns in Central Asia, the U.S. also has a different understanding about China's strategic goals in the region. With the rapid growth of Chinese economic activity in recent years, the U.S. believes that economic interests, especially the demand for Central Asian energy, are the major concern for China in developing its relations with Central Asia. Since China became an oil-importing country in 1996, especially since it became the second oil-consuming country last year, China's dependence on imported oil has kept increasing, and China's oil companies have been seeking new energy markets in the world, including Africa, South America, the Middle East, and Central Asia. The construction of the China-Kazakhstan Oil Pipeline can partly meet China's demand for energy, overcome the fragility of sea transportation, and reduce China's dependence on the Middle East oil.

Further, the U.S. thinks that China's engagement in Central Asia is also out of consideration of its geopolitical strategy. China is on its way to becoming a global power, and is very likely to face challenges from the U.S., Japan and Europe during the process, thus it has to develop a friendly relationship with Central Asian states, in order to foster a stable and conducive environment for its development.

Furthermore, ensuring border security and the stability of Central Asia is a more profound component of China's Central Asia strategy. Because acute conflicts in Central Asia might pose a threat to the security of Xinjiang, the stability of Central Asia means the security of China. In a word, China also holds important security interests in the region.

It can be seen from the above analysis that the order of U.S. priority of concern over China's interests in Central Asia is energy—geopolitics—security. Such an order is in a sense reasonable, for China's demand for energy will remain a key issue in China's economic development in the foreseeable future, as well as an import component of China's foreign policies in recent years. However, different from the U.S. concern of the global strategy in Central Asia, China's major interests in the region lie in regional security, and its order of concerns is very clear too, i.e., regional security—energy—geopolitics. The biggest threat to the security and stability of west China is the "East Turkistan" separatists, as well as the "three forces" in Central Asia. Therefore, China's primary concern in the region is to ensure its stability. In terms of energy and economic interests, China is taking measures to strengthen economic ties with Central Asia, ensure China's access to Central Asian energy, another important source of oil import for China. As to its geopolitical interests, China is endeavoring to prevent Central Asia from being monopolized by any single power in terms of its politics, economy and security. Neither does China expect any traditional big-power competition in Central Asia, nor does it expect the emergence of any hostile force against China in the region.

- From Shanghai 5-State Organization to the SCO

Initially, because both Russia and China expressed their serious concern over the eastward expansion of NATO before the founding of the SCO, worrying that NATO might further extend to Central Asia, the U.S. had a rather incomplete understanding of the impact of the Shanghai 5-State Organization and the SCO on regional security, regarding them as only a tool for China to expand its influence in Central Asia, or for both China and Russia to jointly prevent the U.S. and NATO from entering Central Asia. However, 9/11 happened less than three months after the founding of the SCO, whose member states all gave their active support in the U.S. anti-terrorist war in Afghanistan, which indicates that the SCO is not only aimed against the U.S., but it also has many common interests with the U.S. in anti-terrorism and regional security. Gradually, the U.S. came to realize the significance of the SCO to Central Asia and began its communication and cooperation, so as to maintain regional security with their joint efforts.

China believes that security interests are not only a strong driving force behind the Shanghai 5-State Organization and the SCO, but are a major concern for China in developing its friendly relations with Central Asian states. As China shares over 3,000 kilometers of borders with Kazakhstan, Kyrgyzstan and Tajikistan, as well as many common ethnic groups, China's national interests are closely related to the situation in Central Asia, not only in history, but in reality as well. Among the factors that might affect security and stability in Central Asia, the most pressing issue for China used to be border disputes with Central Asian states. Thus the primary goal of Shanghai 5-State Organization was to complete the border division between China and these states, as well as Russia, and to demilitarize the border areas. In April 1996, heads of China, Russia, Kazakhstan, Kyrgyzstan and Tajikistan attended their first meeting in Shanghai and signed the *Agreement on Strengthening Mutual military trust in the Border Areas*; in April of the following year, they signed the *Agreement on Joint Reduction of Military Forces in the Border Areas* in Moscow. After the solution of border security issues, the five states put combating "the three forces" at the top of their agenda; later, the anti-terrorist military exercises held by SCO members, as well as the establishment of the SCO Counterterrorism Center and the SCO Rapid-Response Counterterrorism Troops, aimed only at preventing the actions of the "three forces" in Central Asia.

China also expects to seek solutions to the "East Turkistan" issues through cooperation with other SCO members. The "East Turkistan Liberation Movement" has had many connections with Central Asia in history, ethnic groups, culture, language and religion. With the drastic change in Central Asian geopolitics after the disintegration of the Soviet Union, the Movement has been increasingly influenced by extremist and terrorist forces: its members set up bases in Central Asia, receive terrorist training in Afghanistan, and receive spiritual support and material aid from other international terrorist organizations, thus forming an active terrorist zone from Chechnya to Central Asia, and then to Xinjiang. Therefore, combating the "East Turkistan" separatist forces, confining their actions to Central Asia, and preventing terrorist forces from entering China, will be the primary goal of China's Central Asia strategy well into the future, for which the SCO has been, and will continue to serve as, an important mechanism.

China-Central Asia cooperation on energy

The U.S. has kept close watch on the energy cooperation between China and the Central Asian states, especially with Kazakhstan and Uzbekistan. According to a report by the Committee on U.S.-China Economy and Security Assessment of the U.S. Congress, China's rapidly increasing demand for energy, especially its dependence on imported oil, will pose challenges to the U.S. in economic activity, the environment and geopolitics. The U.S. believes that the greater the amount of Central Asian oil that is exported to China, the less will be exported to the U.S. and Europe, and it is even afraid of the possibility of U.S.-China conflicts over energy in the future.

China has regarded enhancing cooperation with Central Asian states on energy as an important strategic goal, yet due to the relatively small size of China-controlled oil fields and its limited production capability, China does not obtain very much energy from the region each year, thus posing no threat to the U.S.'s strategy for Central Asian energy. The construction of the China-Kazakhstan Oil Pipeline began in September 2004, but will not be completed until 2011, with an expected annual import of 20 million tons. However, for lack of oil sources, the already-constructed "Pakeye Pipeline" that passes through Azerbaijan must transport at least 20 million tons of Kazakh oil each year to maintain its normal functions, while Kazakh oil output can hardly meet the demands of China-Kazakhstan pipeline, the Pakeye pipeline, and the Russian pipeline at the same time. Hence the possibility of competition between the China-Kazakhstan pipeline and the Pakeye pipeline.

- The geopolitical significance of China's peaceful ascendancy in Central Asia

As a major regional rising power, China must regard the stability of its border areas as a prerequisite for its development, for which purpose China must enhance cooperation with the Central Asian states. Nevertheless, the U.S. attaches great geopolitical significance to China's Central Asia strategy and occasionally expresses serious concern over China's increasing influence in the region, as well as over the geopolitical changes brought about by China's economic ascendancy.

From China's perspective, Central Asia's greatest significance for China's geopolitical strategy is that the region could become a stable back zone of China. Current security pressures on China, as well as China's strategic tasks, mainly come from the southeast, including the Taiwan Strait crises, acute China-Japan conflicts, and the competition over resources in South China Sea. Thus, the security and stability of the western borders is crucial to China's overall security strategy. Moreover, China's strategy is to balance the powers of Russia, the U.S. and the European Union in Central Asia, to prevent any single power from monopolizing the region, and to avoid traditional large-power competition. China's rise does not threaten the Central Asian states, and nor will it harm their interests, not only because the development of China's economy will promote Central Asia's economic development, but because the Central Asian states can learn much from China's experience. Further, China-Central Asia relations are developing within the framework of the SCO. And after Iran, India and Pakistan became observers of the SCO, almost all strong regional powers related to Central Asia have participated in the organization, which to a large extent confines the settlement of any issue concerning regional security and economy.

Common Interests of the U.S. and China, and Prospective Fields of Cooperation

Based on the above analysis of the respective focal concerns of the U.S. and China, it can be concluded that there are no essential interest conflicts between the two nations: China actively supports the U.S. in its primary concern of counter-terrorism, while China's primary concern—the geopolitics of Central Asia and security interests—is not a focal concern of the U.S. Neither poses a challenge to the other's essential interests in Central Asia.

In terms of the overall development of U.S.-China relations, despite their disagreement on such issues as energy and U.S. troops stationed in Central Asia, China and the U.S. are generally enjoying rather good political, military and economic relations, and neither country intends to involve the other in conflicts in Central Asia. On the contrary, both countries share many common interests in the region, including counter-terrorism, combating transnational crime, energy exploitation and cooperation, as well as regional security, among others.

- Common interests of the U.S. and China in Central Asia

Although terrorism ranks differently in the security agendas of the U.S. and China, its presence poses a common threat to both countries in Central Asia. As a neighbor of Central Asia, China has suffered greatly from the "East Turkistan" separatist forces in Xinjiang, who have been threatening the security and stability of west China with the aid of terrorist organizations in Central Asia. Since the U.S. military attacks on the Taliban in Afghanistan after 9/11, Central Asia has moved to the forefront in the battle against international terrorism. Therefore, combating terrorism and maintaining regional security are the most important common shared interests of China and the U.S. after 9/11; counter-terrorism in Central Asia not only accords with U.S. global strategy, but it also helps China contain the "East Turkistan" separatist forces.

The U.S. needs China's support in its counter-terror actions in Central Asia because of China's good relations with Pakistan and its influence in the Central Asian states. Meanwhile, China needs the U.S.' understanding and cooperation in combating "East Turkistan" terrorist forces, which, in turn, contributes to U.S.'s interests in Central Asia. Therefore, both countries have started cooperation since 9/11 on such issues as exchanging information on counter-terrorism, cutting off the financial sources of terrorist organizations, as well as tracking down their money-laundry activities. Moreover, both countries share common interests in fighting transnational crime. Much organized crime, including drug smuggling, arms proliferation, and illegal immigration, is closely related to terrorist forces, and Central Asia is the major passageway for drug smuggling from Afghanistan, which is not only an important source of funds for terrorist organizations, but also relates to arms proliferation. Hence, it is in the interests of both the U.S. and China to combat religious extremist forces in Central Asia, stop their connections with international terrorist forces, block their access to weapons of mass destruction, and prevent their predominance in Central Asia.

Another shared interest between the U.S. and China in Central Asia is to maintain stability and development in the region. The universal political, economic, religious, ethnic and social problems in the Central Asian states not only make it difficult for the states to control terrorism and extremism, but also provide the soil for their growth. Any turmoil in Central Asia can be exploited by terrorist and extremist forces to threaten the security interests of the U.S. and China, thus both countries should help maintain security and enhance prosperity in the region: on the one hand, a stable Central Asia will serve as a better milieu for China's development, and both will benefit in the end; on the other hand, avoiding large-scale turmoil and containing any form of extremism in the region will greatly help guarantee U.S. interests in Central Asia.

Maintaining stability in Central Asia is the responsibility of both the Central Asian states and all other concerned countries. Key internal factors that affect the stability in the region also include territory disputes and conflicts over water resources. As there were no border lines between Central Asian states in Soviet times, and existing lines have only symbolic meaning, territorial disputes are universal among Central Asian states. For example, in Kyrgyzstan, seven lands belong to minority nationalities of other states, five of which are connected to Uzbekistan and two to Tajikistan, which might lead to bitter disputes or even acute conflicts between these states. Further, many conflicts exist in Central Asia over ecological and other resources, especially over water. The two upstream states, Tajikistan and Kyrgyzstan, practically dominate the economic lifeline of downstream states by controlling reservoirs constructed upstream. Recently, Turkmenistan rapidly increased its use of water from the Amu River, resulting in a severe shortage of water in some areas of Uzbekistan. Under such pressures, Central Asian states are calling for help from global and regional powers while also trying to avoid being under the control of any single power. Therefore, China and the U.S. need to join other strong powers in the pursuit for ways to maintain stability in Central Asia.

China and the U.S. also share important common interests in Central Asian energy. It is a common wish of both countries to share oil and natural gas in the region, as well as to avoid conflicts over energy. With the steady economic development of both countries, China and the U.S. both need stable and accountable sources of energy. Thus, their energy cooperation will not only deepen their understanding of each other's energy policies and enhance their communication in the field of energy, but will also promote their cooperation on certain energy projects.

- Field of cooperation between China and the U.S. in Central Asia

China's rising influence in Central Asia does not pose a practical threat to U.S. interests in the region, as China has been endeavoring to set up constructive relations with the U.S. on Central Asian and other security issue in the surrounding areas, so as to create a favorable environment for China's development. However, China and the U.S. differ in their opinions of the political transformation, economic development and energy exploitation in Central Asia, as well as of the U.S. troops in the region. Hence, both countries should further enhance their communication and cooperation, dissolve their misperceptions of each other's strategic goals, and gradually establish mutual military trust. China hopes to expand U.S.-China cooperation in such fields as strengthening the SCO-U.S. ties, establishing strategic mutual military trust with the U.S. to the greatest possible extent, as well as expanding their cooperation in non-traditional security fields.

- The SCO and the U.S.

Due to the complex relationships between the interests of major powers in Central Asia, any attempt to strengthen bilateral relations might have negative effects; only with multilateral cooperation mechanisms that engage all major powers can their cooperation be more effective and transparent. Currently, there exist three important multilateral cooperation organizations in Central Asia, namely the NATO Partnership mechanism, the CIS Collective Security Treaty Organization, and the Shanghai Cooperation Organization: the first involves the U.S., Russia and the Central Asian states; the second involves only Russia and the Central Asian states; and the third involves China, Russia and the Central Asian states—none engages China and the U.S. at the same time. Since the disintegration of the Soviet Union, the U.S. has been playing an active role in Central Asian issues: not only has it started its cooperation with Central Asian states through the NATO Partnership for Peace plan, but they have also strengthened their relationship through joint counter-terrorist actions in the Afghanistan War. The SCO is the most important platform upon which China plays its role in Central Asia. Over the past five years, SCO members have managed to establish mechanisms for multilateral mutual trust, as well as cooperation in regional security, and they are expanding their economic cooperation at present. China expects to promote its cooperation with the U.S. on the basis of the SCO.

Because of important U.S. interests and influence in Central Asia, the future development of the SCO must take the U.S. into account. Under current conditions, two means can be adopted to start SCO-U.S. cooperation: one is cooperation between the two regional international organizations, NATO and the SCO; the other is between the SCO and the U.S. alone. However, the SCO does not match NATO in its functions, bodies, and scale; the issue of the U.S.'s becoming an SCO observer is also to be further discussed, as the organization has been joined by three new observers: India, which is regarded by the U.S. as a strategic partner; Pakistan, a U.S. counter-terrorism ally; and Iran, a standing foe of the U.S. Nevertheless, limited U.S. participation in SCO actions would certainly help increase the position and influence of the SCO.

- The establishment of mutual military trust

There are three anti-terrorist centers now in Central Asia: the U.S. airbases in Uzbekistan and Kyrgyzstan; the Russian airbases in Kyrgyzstan and Tajikistan, and; the SCO Counter-terrorism Center in Uzbekistan. Not only are the three centers relatively independent in military command, but China and Russia have also already begun to worry about the U.S. troops long stationed in Central Asia. Hence the importance of establishing mutual military trust between the U.S. and the SCO members. So far, China and Russia have successfully established mutual military trust within the framework of the SCO and have begun to conduct a few military exercises to combat the "three forces" and achieve mutual security. Only on the basis of mutual military trust can the U.S. troops stationed in Central Asia be regarded as an important force to maintain regional security, instead of a threat.

Due to their different political systems and for ideological reasons, China and the U.S. have not yet established strategic mutual trust. However, the most direct way to establish and consolidate mutual trust is always to continue strengthening military communication and cooperation. Since 9/11, cooperation between the military forces of both countries has begun in the exchange of anti-terrorist intelligence; academic communication is being conducted between their military institutions; both have begun to send observers to the other's military exercises. Moreover, it is necessary to create a crisis-management system in Central Asia, to inform each other before military exercises in Central Asia, as well as to set up hotlines to avoid conflict escalation in times of crisis. Through proper military cooperation and communication, the U.S. and China can develop a better understanding of each other, and gradually establish an effective and transparent cooperation mechanism.

- Cooperation in non-traditional fields

Apart from military communication and cooperation, China and the U.S. share additional prospects in non-traditional security fields. In terms of energy, they can conduct cooperation on information exchange, energy policies and strategy development, as well as on techniques and planning. Other economic and social cooperation is also helpful Central Asia's social stability and economic development, such as helping remove land mines along the borders of Central Asian states, preventing AIDS, improving the infrastructure of Central Asia, as well as setting up schools, hospitals and vocational training centers.

A Brief Conclusion

National interests are the foundation of a country's foreign policies. Mutual respect of each other's national interests is a prerequisite for the acknowledgement of mutual interests, which are the basis for cooperation. The better China and the U.S. understand each other's objectives and policies, the more they will benefit form their bilateral cooperation.

China and the U.S. share a large number of common interests in most fields, which lays a good foundation for their further cooperation, and that, in turn, will enhance their mutual trust. Both countries should try their best to avoid conflicts, with a constructive attitude. We believe that, compared with the fields in which U.S.-China cooperation can be conducted, the fields where they cannot cooperate are rather few, so it is unwise to extend their conflicts in a certain field to other fields where they can cooperate well otherwise.

Some conflicts between China and the U.S. are caused by misperceptions of interests, and others are caused by the influence of their general relationship. Yet compared with Northeast Asia, Southeast Asia, and even South Asia, Central Asia is the region where both countries share the most common interests and prospects for cooperation. If both countries have a better understanding of each other's interests as well as their common interests in Central Asia, they can conduct better cooperation in the region, which will be helpful both to the stability of the region and to the further development of China-U.S. relations.

About the Contributors

Dong Xiaoyang is a professor of Russian studies and deputy director of the Institute of Russian, East European and Central Asian Studies at the Chinese Academy of Social Sciences (CASS) in Beijing. A graduate of Jilin University, Beijing University Law School, and Moscow University, Mr. Dong was a visiting professor at Harvard University Russian Research Center in 1990, and the Russian Research Center of Toronto University in 1991. In 1996 before assuming his current position with CASS he was a senior researcher at the Embassy of China in Moscow. His co-author, **Su Chang**, is assistant professor, Institute of Russian/East European and Central Asian Studies at CASS.

Fu Yong received her Ph.D. in international politics from Fudan University, School of International Studies, in Shanghai in 2005. She is a member of the Shanghai Academy of Social Sciences (SASS), working in the Institute of Eurasian Studies. She received a B.A. and M.A. degree in world history from Changchun University, and has studied at the Center for Chinese and American Studies at Johns Hopkins-Nanjing University.

Brigadier General (retired) **Feroz Khan** served with the Pakistani Army for 30 years. He served domestically and abroad with numerous assignments in the United States, Europe, and South Asia. He has experienced combat action and command on active fronts on the line of control in Siachin Glacier and Kashmir. Most recently, he held the post of Director, Arms Control and Disarmament Affairs, within the Strategic Plans Division, Joint Services Headquarters. Among his academic degrees, General Khan holds an M.A. from the Nitze School of Advanced International Studies.
Since the mid 1990`s General Khan has been making key contributions in formulating and advocating Pakistan's security policy on nuclear and conventional arms control and strategic stability in South Asia. He has produced recommendations for the Ministry of Foreign Affairs and represented Pakistan in several multilateral and bilateral arms control negotiations. He has written and participated in several security-related national and international conferences and seminars and has also been teaching as a visiting faculty member at the Department of the Defense and Strategic Studies, Quaid-e-Azam University, Islamabad.
For the past two years, General Khan has held a series of visiting fellowships at Stanford University's Center for International Studies and Arms Control; the Woodrow Wilson International Center for Scholars; the Brookings Institution; the Center for Non-Proliferation Studies at the Monterey Institute of International Studies; and the Cooperative Monitoring Center, Sandia National Laboratory. General Khan is now a visiting professor of national security affairs at the U.S. Naval Postgraduate School.

Ni Jianping is a post-doctoral research fellow at the School of Journalism, Fudan University in Shanghai, is a research associate at the Shanghai Institute of American Studies, and lectures as an adjunct professor at East China Normal University, School of Communication. He received his Ph.D. in international relations from Fudan University in 2001. He has studied overseas at Hong Kong Baptist University in 1998, and the

Elliott School of International Relations, George Washington University in Washington D.C. in 2000. He has also studied at the Schiller Institute in Germany, and at Moscow State University.

Pan Guang is the director and professor of the Shanghai Center for International Studies, and the Institute of European and Asian Studies at the Shanghai Academy of Social Sciences; director of the SCO (Shanghai Cooperation Organization) Studies Center in Shanghai; and dean of the Center of Jewish Studies Shanghai (CJSS) and vice-chairman of the Chinese Society of Middle East Studies. He is professor of History and Political Science, and the Walter and Seena Fair professor for Jewish and Israeli Studies. He is an International Council member of the Asia Society in the USA, senior advisor of the China-Eurasia Forum in the USA, and an advisory board member of the Asia Europe Journal in Singapore. He has traveled and lectured widely in North America, East Asia, Russia, Europe, Middle East and Australia.

Shi Ze graduated from the Russian Department of Xi'an Foreign Language Institute. From 1980 to 1983 he studied for a master's degree in world history in the History Department of Peking University. He was director of the Soviet Union and Eastern Europe Division and the Division of International Politics, and vice-president of the China Institute for International Studies. He served as first secretary in the Chinese Embassy in the Soviet Union and Russia, and as political counselor of the Chinese Embassies in Kazakhstan and Tajikistan. His research areas cover relations between great powers, issues on Europe and Asia, Russia and Central Asia and the Caspian Sea, as well as Chinese western peripheral security. Mr. Shi enjoys the government's "distinguished contributor" specialist allowance.

Sun Zhuangzhi is director of the Central Asian Department of the Institute for East European, Russian and Central Asian Studies, and secretary-general of the Center for Shanghai Cooperation Organization Studies, at the Chinese Academy of Social Sciences (CASS) in Beijing. He studied for his bachelor's and master's degrees in history at Nankai University in Tianjin, and received his Ph.D. in international relations from the Graduate School of CASS in 2000. He has been a visiting scholar at Tashkent University in Uzbekistan, and a senior visiting scholar at Baku State University in Azerbaijan.

Yang Shu is vice president of Lanzhou University, director of its Institute for Central Asian Studies, and a professor in the Department of International Politics. He received his bachelor's and master's degrees in geology from Lanzhou University in 1982 and 1984. From 1988 to 1991 he was second secretary, Department of Education, Chinese Embassy to the Soviet Union. He also holds the post of vice-president of the Chinese Society of East European, Russian and Central Asia Studies and is director of the society's Center for Central Asian Studies. He also consults to the China Academy of Social Sciences on Central Asian issues.

Yu Jianhua is currently professor and deputy director of the Institute of Eurasian Studies, Shanghai Academy of Social Sciences (SASS). In 1988 he received is master's degree in history from the Department of History, East China Normal University. He studied world history and international politics at the Institute of History and Institute of Eurasian Studies, SASS, prior to becoming a visiting exchange fellow at the International Institute for Asian Studies, the Netherlands, in Spring 2002. He received his Ph. D. from the College of Law and Political Science, ECNU. His other positions include: Dean of the Center of Nontraditional Security Studies (SASS), Standing Council member of the Chinese Association for World Ethnic Studies, general secretary of Shanghai Society of World History Studies, Standing Council member of Shanghai Society of International Relations Studies and the Committee member of Shanghai Youth Federation. His major research fields are: issues in the Middle East and Central Asia; nationalism and ethnic conflict; international energy politics; terrorism; and international security.

Zhang Guihong is associate professor of international relations, director of the Program on International Organization and Security (PIOS), and deputy director of the Institute of International Studies, Zhejiang University (IIS/ZJU), Hangzhou, China. He has a Ph.D. from the Center for American Studies, School of International Studies, Fudan University (CAS/SIS/FDU), Shanghai, China. He participated in the Sino-U.S. Summer Workshop on International Security (1996, 1997, 2002); the International Workshop on International Political Economy and Regionalism in the Asia Pacific (1998, 2000) supported by the Program for International Studies in Asia (PISA); the Ninth Workshop on Defense, Technology and Cooperative Security in South Asia (2002) organized by Regional Center for Strategic Studies (RCSS), Sri Lanka; and the International Visitor Program (2003) sponsored by U.S. Department of State. He has also been a visiting scholar at the Henry L. Stimson Center, Washington D.C., USA (2002-2003); and ASIA Fellow at School of International Studies, Jawaharlal Nehru University (SIS/JNU) as well as Institute for Defence Studies and Analyses (IDSA), New Delhi, India (2004-2005). His major areas of research are Sino-US-Indian relations and Asia-Pacific security. His co-author, **Jaideep Saikia**, is a fellow scholar from New Delhi, India.

Zhao Huasheng is director of the Center for Russia and Central Asia Studies at Fudan University in Shanghai. He specializes in Russian foreign policy and security, Sino-Russian relations, Sino-Central Asian relations, and the Shanghai Cooperation Organization. He has twice been a visiting scholar at the Moscow Institute of International Relations, and has written extensively on Russian foreign policy. Recent publications include “China and America in Russia's Foreign Policy,” in *Contemporary International Relations*, and “The Situation in Central Asia and the Shanghai Cooperation Organization,” in *East Europe and Central Asia Studies*. He was previously director of Russian and Central Asian Studies at the Shanghai Institute for International Studies (SIIS) and is currently a senior advisor for the China-Eurasia Forum.

www.ingramcontent.com/pod-product-compliance
Lightning Source LLC
LaVergne TN
LVHW061222100826
845148LV00004B/831

* 9 7 8 1 7 8 0 3 9 0 4 7 5 *